"YES, BUT—"

The Bankruptcy of Apologetics

"YES, BUT—"

The Bankruptcy of Apologetics

By

WILLARD L. SPERRY

Dean of the Theological
School in Harvard University

NEW YORK AND LONDON

Harper & Brothers Publishers

1931

To

L. P. J.

CONTENTS

"YES, BUT—"

The Bankruptcy of Apologetics

CHAPTER ONE

The Religion of "Yes, But—"

———————————— ‹‹›› ————————————

In an early chapter of his *Quest of the Historical Jesus* Schweitzer describes a certain German theologian of the mid-eighteenth century, Johann Semler of Halle, as the "father of the 'yes, but' theology."

Semler had lived to see the beginnings of the historical criticism of the gospels. As a scholar he could not deny the validity of the method, yet as a devout believer he feared its consequences for the faith. He therefore proposed to take back with his pious right hand the concessions which he saw were to be required of his critical left hand. Schweitzer reduces this devious mental process to the brief formula, "yes, but—."

Although Semler is long dead and forgotten, his type of mind persists and is still a grave liability for religion. Persons who profess and call themselves Christians are by that profession committed to doctrines which derive from a remote past. Since the days when the faith was first given, a vast amount of new knowledge has accrued to the world's store of truth and much of this knowledge is in form, if not in substance, incompatible with the ideas of God, man, nature, and history which are found in the primitive gospel. With the passing of time this discrepancy increases and finally creates for the believer a serious dilemma. If he keeps the letter of the old faith he becomes an anachronism, if he casts his lot with the new knowledge he breaks with a precious past. Unless he and his religion are to be outmoded he must eventually make a place within his creed for truths found since the faith was first given. He accepts, therefore, the necessity for a periodic restatement of religion and hopes that the knowledge which is new may be so accommodated to tradition that it will not impair the faith which is old. This is the situation which still invites and seems to warrant the employment of Semler's formula, "yes, but—."

The resulting restatement is never satisfactory, since there lingers about it a hint of casuistry in the process and of compromise in the conclusion. The religious mind does not like to qualify its beliefs and the scientific mind does not care to qualify its truths. The new ideas, which religion admits after a long period of timidity, have been for years the commonplaces of knowledge and the outside world does not see that religion deserves any credit for grudgingly conceding at a late date truths which it should have gladly welcomed from the first. Meanwhile the accommodation of old dogmas to new truths imposes upon the body of doctrine meanings which are quite foreign to it, and subtly alters the whole intellectual content of religion. Thus we may read into the Book of Genesis the doctrine of evolution and into the healing miracles of Jesus our modern psychotherapy, but this is not what the writer of Genesis intended nor what Jesus thought he was doing. The words remain the same, yet they no longer mean what they first meant.

The position of the religionist is not in these matters an enviable one. So far from being a person whose faith rests comfortably upon the support of congenial fact he is more like the Indian fakir lying down upon his bed of nails. Whichever way he turns, sharp facts press painfully upon the body of his beliefs. The non-religious world looks on in perplexity and cannot understand why those who profess religion should prolong this mental self-torture. The believer himself is not without his moments of misgiving in which he wonders whether the Wisdom and Spirit of the Universe requires of him, in the name of religion, such unnatural violence to the forthright processes of thought. At times he is invaded by the heretical suspicion that he may not have identified rightly the realities at issue and that possibly he might achieve a much truer religion by emancipating himself from his bondage to tradition.

In one of his novels Mark Rutherford says of its hero and heroine, "Zachariah and Pauline were private persons; they were, happily for them, committed to nothing, and were not subsidized by their reputations to defend a system." The traditionalist often envies such happy persons their freedom, which by contrast makes him acutely aware of his own forsworn and subsidized state. There are times when he longs for free thought, thought that takes place immediately in the presence of its subject without reference to hereditary doctrines which at all costs must be preserved.

There is something to be said for trying to make a modern religion out of the genius of pure science, since many of the unmercenary tempers of mysticism find their best expression today in the dispassionateness of the sciences. What we know as the scientific method is, as Christianity once was, "a way," a manner of thought before it is a conclusion to thinking. The method antedates the result, and confidence in the validity of the result rests upon prior faith in the integrity of the processes by which it is reached. Something of this sort would seem to be the elusive genius of Protestantism. Along this way there is constant interest; the scientist does not grudgingly concede the advent of new truths, he expects and invites them. He never has to reconcile himself to fresh discoveries since he is not forsworn to any single theory of the universe or subsidized by his profession to defend that theory against all comers. He is habitually prepared to revise even the most familiar and beloved hypothesis in the presence of evidence which points in another direction. In the candor and courage of such inquiry, in its moral integrity and trust that the universe will reveal its truth to those who seek it aright, there are many of the tempers of religion at its best. We feel instinctively that thinking of this kind, rather than labored defence of tradition, should give to religion its body of ideas.

The mind of man has journeyed far in these last two thousand years, latterly with rapid acceleration. Much of the reliable information as to nature and history that we now employ for the conduct of daily life was no part of the primitive gospel, and many of the specific issues which we must meet are not anticipated in the sources. Ultimately we have to take the responsibility for our lives in our own hands and muster courage to call our souls our own. An old man once said to me, "The longer I live the more I am impressed by the reticence of God." We feel this divine reticence when we read our Bibles. In our perplexity we turn the pages of the Gospels, expecting some decisive word, and are baffled by the silences. A modern critic tells us that Walt Whitman seems always to be saying, "I am going away now, and I must leave it to you." The voices from the New Testament seem to be saying just that, and what they leave us is not so much a finished revelation as the opportunity for a first-hand religious life.

Meanwhile the long history of the restatement of religious belief is not pleasant reading. Organized religion has habitually opposed the advent of new truth and has defended both the finality and sufficiency of its own body of doctrine. Therefore churches have got into the wrong relation to the world and there is much ground for Höffding's sobering statement that whereas formerly religion was the pillar of cloud by day and of fire by night which marched in the vanguard of history, now it is merely an ambulance corps which trails along in the rear of the conflict, caring for the sick and wounded. Very few Americans who enlisted in the French or English ambulance service from 1914 to 1917 were content to stay in the ambulance after the spring of '17. So in our moments of holy impatience we ask to be transferred "from the safe glad rear to the dreadful van" of human thought as it fares into the mystery of things. All that is bold and honest in us responds to the unequivocal "yes" of pure science and is increasingly irked by the cautious theological "but" which at present is used to save religion.

There are, however, some values which escape the meshes of the scientific net, and the traditional Christian is not without a case. Take away Christianity with its Bible, and many of the laws, much of the art, most of the history of the Western World, become unintelligible. The purely secular rewriting of that history as a matter of the economic struggle and the class war deprives it of those emotionally charged religious ideas which wrote most of it in the first instance. The official acts of the church are in this respect less important than the subterranean stream of personal piety that has flowed beneath the centuries. All the gentler and more liberal aspects of our civilization have been watered by that stream. In so far as tares have appeared in what Piers Plowman called this "Fair Field Full of Folk," those tares have grown by drawing upon loyalties that were lovely in their Christian origin. The tragedy of our history is precisely this exploiting of an unlimited capacity for devotion and sacrifice in the interest of worldly ends, which have been skillfully disguised as occasions for religion. If Christians in the past have been content to be harmless as doves,

Christians in the future must aspire to become wise as serpents.

Meanwhile there is no present ground for despair of Christianity. As for its ideals for our humanity in general, they are the pronouncement of a bold hope rather than a record of achieved fact. We fall much too easily into the mood of bitter irony which Browning's Fra Lippo Lippi voiced when he looked out over his world and then up at the crucifix to say, "Whose sad face on the cross sees only this after the passion of a thousand years." This is sentimentalism, not sober science, and there is no ground for this pessimism in any realistic account of the processes of nature and history. It is now fifty thousand years since man crawled out of his caves to begin his ascent, and the Christian religion has been dealing with him for only a late fraction of that time. Mandell Creighton was right in saying that after we have got rid of the ape and the tiger we shall have to get rid of the donkey, a much more intractable animal. The patient processes of time are an effort to exorcise the residual wild ass in us all. Given man's imperious brute inheritance, the wonder is not that Christianity has done so little with him, but that it has done so much.

There is, further, an ineradicable strain of poetry in all religion, which may not be denied. Many thinkers of the first rank have not hesitated to say that the truth of poetry is truth of a higher order than that of fact, and that there are aspects of reality which are not accounted for in the main industry of the scientific mind, that of "grinding general laws out of large collections of fact." Darwin, who thus described his life as a biologist, was the first to confess the limitations of this method of arriving at truth and the loss to character when it is employed as the sole avenue to reality. Discipline in scientific thinking has made all of us increasingly impatient of sentimental evasion of fact, yet this discipline ought not to deny us the soul of art. A purely scientific religion, void of the artist's insights and creations, would be a very impoverished religion. It may well be that the adoration of the Virgin, which is a highly poetical concern, is as legitimate and valuable an employment for the human mind as the current realistic inquiries into the physiological and psychological vagaries of persons whose chief claim to interest lies in their indifference to the ideal of chastity. At least we have no advance assurance that the psychoanalytic account of the one will bring us any nearer to ultimate reality than the poetic adoration of the other.

In this area science has only one right; it may and indeed must insist that the truth of poetry shall not do actual violence to truths of fact. At this point theology has yet to learn the lesson which great art has already learned, that the poet may not make the sun rise in the west and set in the east, much as this arrangement might suit his fancy. The valid insights of imagination may not contravene the truth of those facts to which the imagination addresses itself. So neither may religion require us to believe that shadows are in the habit of going back ten degrees upon sun dials to fortify the flagging faith of believers. If such Old Testament statements, or misstatements, of fact cause us little trouble, there are in the hereditary body of doctrine other accounts of fact, lying much nearer the center of our faith, which it is equally difficult to square with what we now know about nature and history. At this point most religious persons become cautious and their mental processes devious. "The trouble with your profession," a doctor once said to me, "is that it is not as honest as mine." That is a sweeping charge to bring against the Christian ministry, yet it is not without warrant, since far too many of us are sprung from Semler's loins, and greet the unequivocal "yes" by which the modern mind responds to truths of fact with the reservations of religion's cautious "but."

Theology has elaborated the ways of saying "but" into the substance of a recognized profession, that of the apologist. In classical Greek, where the word originates, an *apologia* is a reply given personally by a defendant in court to the charge brought against him by the prosecution. "The word has never quite lost this connotation of standing on the defensive." Plato's *Apology* of Socrates is one of the noblest documents of all time, and the situation implied by the dialogue requires that term and no other. The task to which the Christian apologists of the second century addressed themselves was a proper one; Justin and Tatian were clearing their religion of the wanton charges of cannibalism and sexual immorality brought against it by the pagan world, as well as of the prevalent rumor that this religion had nothing to say to intelligent persons. Newman's *Apologia*, though it betrays its author's theological timidity, was a wholly warranted reply to Kingsley's stupid attack upon the author's personal integrity. When, however, we come to Bruce's *Apologetics; or Christianity Defensively Stated*, with its candid attempt to "succour distressed faith," we are not only in the modern world, we are in a highly unsatisfactory world.

Religion must always defend itself against its historic adversaries, the world, the flesh, and the devil, and every healthy religion knows that in this ceaseless warfare the best defense is an aggressive offense. The moral apologetics of Christianity has been truly defined as the expulsive power of a new affection. On the other hand, religion ought not to have to be defended against the honest endeavors of the human mind to discover what is so, and this is precisely the sorry service for which the professional apologist is drafted. Conventional apologetics is usually a business of proving that natural scientists, historians, psychologists, and the like, are wrong and that tradition is right. When concessions as to truth of fact are wrung from the reluctant apologist, the "spiritual values" are to be recovered by use of that one word without which the profession is helpless, its serviceable "but—."

Now is any religion that has to be defended against the search for truth, wherever and however conducted, worth professing and preserving? Within the ranks of conventional religionists no one asks this question, yet it is the one question that ought to be asked. The day has gone when the rhetorical summons to rally to the defense of hearth and home meets instant response. Our hearths and homes have been dragged into too many controversies with which they have no concern. We wish to know whether hearth and home are threatened before we allow ourselves to be conscripted for their defense, and whether those whom we are called to fight off have any malice in their hearts.

Furthermore we notice, in other areas of life, that the great classics are not kept alive by a caste of apologists. The Acropolis, the "Mona Lisa," the Mass in B Minor, "Paradise Lost" do not seem to need defenders. We see to it that there shall always be in the world persons capable of rendering or interpreting all these; we do not raise up a professional class to safeguard them, since they are never in such extremity that they must be succored. Why should we employ in the service of religion a method which we know to be superfluous in these other instances? Have not matters come to a grave pass with religion when its body of idea must be defended against the honest brain-work of the modern world? Either Christianity is not what we have supposed it to be, a religion that stands in its own right, or we are in the wrong relation to it.

There is in one of L. P. Jacks' earlier books a ringing passage which describes the mental temper of those who in the name of religion have overcome the world. They were not the apologists:

There is a moment in the act of worship when neither the prayer of contrition nor the hymn of adoration will satisfy, when the Will breaks the leash of constraint with which the understanding has held it back, and launches itself in triumphant affirmation, and with the full force of its argument within it, against all that is irrational, dark, or terrible in the world. The precautions of self-defence are now abandoned; the baggage train is emptied and left behind; the soul ceases to parley with Principalities and Powers, and, with a joy that is free from all fetters, lifts on high the battle hymn of its faith with the deep refrain of "I believe." . . . Religion, no longer entrenched behind bulwarks, is now seen marching into the open, like an army with banners, the Ark of the Covenant in the midst, and the trumpeters going on before.

Isaiah and Jesus had no other conception of Religion than this. They spake with authority, and the note of triumph was in their voices. When they argued, it was unto conviction. The sense of power, dependent on no temporal suffrage whatsoever, rings out in every prophet's cry. The attitude of self-defence is foreign to the prophet; he must always attack; must always be of good cheer; must always go forth conquering and to conquer. The attitude of self-defence is foreign even to the makers of the ancient Creeds. . . . Theirs was not the spirit of spurious open-mindedness, so much in fashion nowadays, which worships a note of interrogation,—the timidity which dares commit itself to nothing. . . . The lines have fallen to us in a highly apologetic age. The dogmatism of the creeds is bad, this other extreme is worse. How can the world fail to despise a religion which is accompanied by a perpetual excuse for its own existence?*

Our Oxford friend has here touched us on the quick. Consider the lot of the ordinary Christian who holds faithfully to tradition and yet must go abroad into the world of today. He no longer expects, on the strength of his religious beliefs, to be counted a necessary member of the thoughtful society in which

* L. P. Jacks, *The Alchemy of Thought*. Williams and Norgate. pp. 318-20.

he mingles. His friends in this wider world tolerate him genially, they do not seem to need the help of his creed for the doing of their work. He observes that much of the serious work of the world, particularly in research fields and in the professions, is being done and in the main well done without the aid of those ideas which he thinks of as distinctively Christian. If his contemporaries are making use of religion in their work it is some subtle temper which cannot be identified with the dogmas he has inherited and still professes. The trouble is that he cannot see that the addition of these dogmas to the mental and moral outfit of his fellows would mean more useful or more skillful work in philosophy, history, medicine, or law. If he is a candid person he will admit that when men are trying to find the cause and cure of cancer or to define more justly the disputed boundaries between newly formed states in eastern Europe, there is no clear revelation on these matters in Christian tradition; yet this is the sort of task which recruits the best minds and evokes the hardest thinking of our day. The difficulty is that in so many of these affairs his hereditary religion seems not so much mistaken as irrelevant.

If his world were uniformly peopled by bad men doing poor work, the contribution his religion might make would be plainer. What perplexes him is just the fact that there are so many good men doing such skillful and useful work, who seem to get along quite well without dogmatic Christianity. Our religionist, therefore, cannot escape a certain natural resentment that his type of mind seems so superfluous, and this sense of being increasingly left out of the tasks that the world is working hardest at, throws him more and more onto the defensive in behalf of his faith. Now all this is not as it should be and something is very wrong here. May it be, not that religion is outworn nor that the environing world is wicked, but that the man who professes religion today is not in the right relation to religion and to his world?

In the preface to his volume, *Reality*, Canon Streeter makes just this suggestion. He says that as he looks back over his life he sees that for years he has been asking the wrong question; he has asked, "Is Christianity true?" The fixed habit of approaching religion through this question, he goes on to say, has put him in an entirely mistaken relation to all that should be meant by religion, since it implies that Christianity is itself a question, whereas it was at first intended to be and ought still to be the answer to a question. When the logic of life runs true, the world and our experiences in that world ask the question and religion proposes the answer. Thus the modern Christian, having begun by asking the wrong question, or by putting the question in the wrong place, has become a defender of the faith and "has got himself into the position of being anxious to save religion, instead of expecting religion to save him." Canon Streeter therefore parts company, in writing of Reality, with the whole science of apologetics, and makes no attempt either to vindicate or to defend Christianity. He opens his mind to those truths which are borne in upon it as he stands in the presence of what seems to be indubitably so, and he lets tradition take the consequences. Now this is the experience of an acute and courageous mind with far more than the ordinary capacity for self-knowledge. And there is no doubt that in identifying the seat of his own religious difficulty, Canon Streeter has done much to help the rest of us understand our dilemma.

Coleridge once said, "He who begins by loving Christianity better than truth, will proceed by loving his own sect or church better than Christianity, and end by loving himself better than all." Most of our present religious perplexities arise from the false assumption that it is possible to love Christianity better than truth. This assumption is false because what is so loved cannot be a religion. It is precisely because so many unthinking Christians today believe that it is possible to love Christianity better than the truth that there is the sorry schism between loyalty to faith and devotion to truth with which we are all too familiar.

Alas, nine persons out of ten who profess and call themselves Christians do not believe that no man ever suffered religious hurt in knowing the truth. They still hold that if some newly discovered or formulated truth is incompatible with statements embedded in religious tradition, it is incumbent upon them to ignore the truth and hold the faith. We are told in the Fourth Gospel that our most precious heritage from Jesus is a spirit dwelling within us that shall lead us into all truth, and that is the very point at which faith sticks. The Christian church has never been quite clear what it means by the Holy Spirit; even the most zealous advocates of high Trinitarianism hold the vaguest theories of this Third Person. We might say, in a moment of wry humor, that the science and practice of apologetics rest upon a basic scepticism as to the presence in the minds of men of any divine spirit that is seeking to lead them into all truth.

Contemporary Christianity, if it is ever to be rid of the timidity betrayed by its apologetic tempers, needs a realistic doctrine of the Spirit. We must believe that wherever men are honestly trying to find out what was so or what is so, there we are to discern the promptings and leadings of the indwelling Word of God. There is no reason to qualify this faith with any cautious "but ——." We concede that particular inquiries within restricted scientific areas are often wholly untheological in their premises and tentatively agnostic in their conclusions, yet this is no reason for fearing or ignoring them. It cannot be otherwise, given the highly specialized nature of most of the intensive intellectual work of the modern world. The climbers on Mount Everest said that when they were moving on the upper slopes of the mountain they had little time or inclination to "enjoy the view." The laborious business of breathing and of taking the next step on a safe foothold absorbed their whole attention. Much of our exacting modern thinking is conducted under similar conditions and we may not criticize for their want of a comprehensive theology men whose minds must be fixed intently upon a very restricted field unless they are to imperil their inquiry and invalidate their conclusions by error in the succession of their mental steps. What matters is their integrity and scrupulous attention to the business in hand. We may not disparage and dismiss them when they return from their ascent because they have not brought back a clear impression of the entire cosmic landscape or an inclusive doctrine of God. We would generously acknowledge the particular and difficult task they have accomplished.

The seeker after truth should have from organized religion its whole confidence and generous encouragement. If he goes about his work today with an inherited prejudice against religion that is because religion in the past has denied him the right to work unfettered in his own field and has so defined itself as to exclude his concern. Churches have only themselves to thank for the tacit hostility or frank indifference which they meet from many of the best minds of our own time. They have too often identified religious faith with erroneous statements of fact brought down by tradition from a remote past and left lying problematically in our world like the boulders of a terminal moraine. Many of these "facts" never happened and others have been misinterpreted. The case for religion is lost if it is mainly a matter of dogged fidelity to misstatements or misinterpretations of happenings in nature and history. Living religion will be taken away from persons who so construe the case and given to others who have a realistic belief in the Holy Spirit.

What we have been saying amounts to this, that we must set about ridding ourselves of the all but fixed mental habit of thinking about faith and knowledge with the aid of the vicious formula "yes, but ———." The employment of that formula has already alienated from us much of the best thinking of the last century, and we begin to suspect that, so far from saving us our religion, it may be costing us our religion. This indictment holds not merely of orthodox theology, it applies equally, though in different manner, to liberal thought. For liberalism, even if it has little interest in defending historic dogmas, is anxiously concerned to save religion itself. The meager word "but" by which this end is supposed to be achieved is not, as the apologist would have us suppose, fuel for the flagging beacon of faith; it is the bushel that hides and finally puts out the light. When invoked, it marks the beginning of the end, as a stimulant for the feeble pulse of conviction, an opiate to deaden the final pain of utter unbelief.

It is not enough to consent in abstract theory to the proposition that there is a Holy Spirit which leads men into all truth; this faith must be proved by works. Christianity must enter with confidence and without reservation into every honest endeavor to find out what is so, and in the presence of the fact or truth must speak an unequivocal "yes." Wherever this high transaction of truth-seeking and truth-finding takes place there, if only we had the courage to believe it, is also "the mind of Christ." If there must always remain something for religion to add to particular findings, that addition is not to be construed as a qualification. Religion may exist to fulfill what men know; it does not exist to refute what they know. For as the wise man said long since, the holy spirit of truth is one in kind.

CHAPTER TWO

The Theology of "Religion and—"

--------------------------------〈〈〉〉--------------------------------

Religion nowadays seldom appears alone in public; it is habitually in company with some other human concern. We meet it thus as Religion and Science, Religion and Art, Religion and Business, Religion and the State, Religion and the Home. Since the society that it thus keeps is above reproach, we do not question the propriety of its manners. Something has happened to religion, however, or to our understanding of it, that we so habitually think of it in connection with these other interests.

If we try to find out why these yoked words are so common we shall probably be driven to the conclusion that they are a disguise for the old apologetic "yes, but—." Despite its cheerful initial intimations the phrase "religion and—" betrays a desire to save something, in this instance religion itself. Our time has a childlike trust in its own phrase-making, and the power of those phrases to solve all mysteries. The truth is that the formula "religion and—" is the admission of a perplexity, not its resolution.

The use of this formula probably arose as a protest against the departmental views of life from which we suffer. In the Middle Ages men saw life steadily and saw it whole to a degree that since those happy times has been denied us. The bishops who designed and the stone-cutters who built the cathedrals of Europe would never have construed their work as ventures in religion and architecture or religion and masonry; their life was an undifferentiated whole. They could not have told you where religion left off and where drawing plans or laying stones began.

In place of that enviable wholeness of life we have today the single striking successes and the total cultural dilemma of specialization. Of this world of divided endeavors an Oxford philosopher says:

This is the fruit of the Renaissance. If the artist, or the priest, or the philosopher complains, we can only answer, "Tu l'as voulu, George Dandin." He demanded freedom and he has got it. He wanted a real separation, art for art's sake, truth for truth's sake, religion for religion's sake, each free from all claims on the part of the rest; and now the freedom has come home to roost, in the form of that disruption of life which we analysed at the beginning. In the middle ages the artist may not have been much of an artist, the philosopher was by our standards only mildly philosophical, and the religious man not extremely religious; but they were all men, whole of heart and secure in their grasp on life. Today we can be as religious as we please, but we cannot ever be men at all; we are wrecks and fragments of men, and we do not know where to take hold on life and how to begin looking for the happiness which we know we do not possess.

What is wrong with us is precisely the detachment of these forms of experience—art, religion, and the rest—from one another; and our cure can only be their reunion in a complete and undivided life. . . . In a sense, that is to say, we demand that the work of the Renaissance shall be undone. . . . It is the fundamental principle of Christianity that the only life worth living is the life of the whole man, every faculty of body and soul unified into a single organic system.*

So construed, the present habit of saying, "religion and ——," would seem to be a deliberate attempt to get back of the age of specialization to the lost unity of human life. The process often has more of the quality of a mechanical reassembly of scattered parts than the reanimation of an organic whole, nevertheless the phrase has a specious note of promise. The significance of the formula lies in the constancy of its first member, since it seems to imply a general agreement that, among our many and often widely diverse interests, religion is best qualified to serve as the liaison officer between them all. We thus require of modern religion that it shall keep open a "House of the Interpreter" where specialists who are suffering from the existing confusion of

* R. G. Collingwood, *Speculum Mentis*. Oxford University Press. pp. 34, ff.

tongues shall be able to communicate with one another on the basis of their common humanity. Religion speaks no technical jargon; when witnessing to what is most characteristic of itself it uses those elemental words which every man understands.

Nevertheless, the full implications of the formula "religion and—" are by no means reassuring. The words plainly imply that matters have been going none too well with religion itself and that a suitable marriage of convenience with some other substantial interest would be desirable. Facing the prospect of dying without issue, religion proposes to confer its Cophetuan dignities upon the beggarly elements of the world. Those beggarly elements, being latterly in much distress, welcome the glad annunciation that they have been elected the handmaidens of a peculiar piety. Prudential considerations operate with equal force on both sides. The French have a name for such negotiations; they call them "powder in the eyes," since they obscure the true situation. And indeed these cultural nuptials between our religion and our other concerns usually lack the lyric quality of an indubitable love affair; they suggest rather the mutual poverty of circumstance that has prompted them. It may be quite wise and well to try to deliver our human interests from their isolation, yet we should not be too hastily betrayed by the seductive theory, which remains to be vindicated in experience, that it is cheaper for two poor persons to live together than apart. In particular, since the use of the conjunction "and" is only one of the mechanical devices by which historic religion has tried to unify life, it is worth our while, in passing, to consider the classical alternatives.

The formula "religion or—" has much to commend it. Religion ought to be, if William James is right, a forced, momentous option. All religions which lay stress on the grim reality of the moral struggle tend to state their case in this way. No militant religion has ever said, "religion and—"; it has always said, "religion or—." This latter formula has, however, certain liabilities; in particular its proponents are apt to proffer a trivial rather than a genuinely momentous option. Sectarian religion has an unhappy flair for fastening on irrelevancies, and while the denominational zealot may be dead in earnest, the world has too often suffered from his meager fanaticism. These forced trivial options have uniformly ushered in the ages of intolerance and persecution. By contrast the ages of tolerance may seem unheroic and stained with moral compromise, yet the memory of the unnecessary suffering which religious fanaticism has cost the world disinclines our time to turn the formula "religion or—" into an engine of some modern inquisition.

In times of moral discouragement, when the world has been so much with them as to become too much for them, men have tended to say, "religion minus—." This formula is the prelude to asceticism, which proposes to achieve unity of life by the drastic putting out of the offending eye and the remorseless cutting off of the too vagrant hand. A sound initial case can always be made for ascetic religion. Certain situations arise in life which offer a man little more than the hope that he may escape with his soul inviolate and still his own. At such times the concern for personal spiritual integrity is neither selfishness nor private right; it is the essence of social duty, since the virtue of persons who thus renounce the world becomes the saving remnant that begets a better world to follow. The late Canon Bigg of Oxford used to tell his classes in church history that no one had any right to criticize the cult of dirt which prevailed among the first Christian hermits of the Egyptian desert in the early centuries, unless he thoroughly understood the moral connotation of taking a bath in the Alexandria of that day! There is no rhetorical exercise safer and shabbier than that in which many moderns indulge, putting up the ascetic man of straw for the fun of knocking him down with their philistine healthy-mindedness. The ascetic is parodied from the outset and is never allowed to appear in his own authentic, austere person. One glance at the familiar profile portrait of Savonarola should be enough to stop this poor sport.

Yet, simple as the ascetic solution of life's riddle is, it has remained the lot of the few, not the vocation for the many. The churches which still defend the "religious" life, so construed, have a double ethic which concedes less exacting requirements for those who must continue to live in the world. Furthermore, we now know enough about the promptings to asceticism and certain of its consequences to realize that psychologically this life is not as ideal as men have supposed it to be. Asceticism often springs from perversions and is strangely liable to subsequent aberration and degeneration. As a rule of life for all sorts and conditions of men it remains yet to be vindicated.

The formula "religion in—" offers a far more serviceable method of achieving unity of life and has the advantage of substituting a qualitative account of religion for the cruder quantitative accounts implied by the formulas, "religion and—" . . . "religion or—" . . . "religion minus—." So defined, religion is not a clearly differentiated human concern, to which other interests may be added or from which they may be subtracted; it is the leaven hidden in the lump, the heat diffused through the iron in the fire.

This was the interpretation of the relation of Christianity to culture proposed by the Roman Catholic Modernists of twenty-five years ago. They saw religion as a spirit inhabiting and inspiring a wild profusion of ideas and interests. "Christianity," says Tyrrell, speaking of its earlier history, "was not a religion, but a spirit, mode, or quality of religion, which might be found in various religions, but never apart by itself as a 'subsistent quality.' " His favorite simile, which he used to describe the way in which the gospel entered the ancient world, was that of the oil from the widow's cruse poured into the empty vessels gathered from the neighbor world, which ceased to flow only when there was not a vessel more. Thus the elaboration of Catholic piety is not to the Modernist, as it is to the Protestant, a progressive degradation of the gospel; it is rather a proof of the intense vitality of the gospel.

Liberal Protestantism has been trying to get back of this Catholic elaboration to recover the simple evangelical piety of the gospels, and Catholic Modernism must seem to all who share in this endeavor mere special pleading in behalf of Rome. Protestantism suspects and deplores the long succession of pagan myths become Christian dogmas and local deities turned Christian saints, which we find in the Catholic record; it covets the freshness of some early uncorrupted world. Yet that world has been very hard to recover, and in so far as found has not proved uniformly intelligible or serviceable to our time. Our long backward leap ignores the living logic of history which has brought us to the present hour. Despite the patent difficulties involved, the Catholic Modernist reading of the way in which Christianity is related to history has the advantage of conceding to the gospel from the first, and of preserving until now, its intense vitality. Biologically and sociologically it seems more likely to be a faithful account of the facts than is to be had from any other available theory. Things fell out that way because such is the nature and manner of life itself. If, therefore, we must make formulas to help religion, this last would seem to be the best.

Yet when we have said all this there remains a margin of wintry discontent, as though we were trying to make the best of a bad case. Religion is not well served by these random particles of speech. These mechanical aids to thought, by which we try to relate religion to the world, all suggest qualifying or minimizing turns of mind which are alien to the spiritual principle we wish to affirm. Surely this word "religion" is an imperial word that should stand alone, needing no props. The attempt to compound it with other words succeeds only in compromising it. Should we not cultivate the power to think and say this word in its singleness, since this of all words in the language should be no stranger to the "self-sufficing power of solitude"?

Thus, no modern man with any feeling for the past can stand on the high terrace at Mont-Saint-Michel, looking up at the church behind him, down at the rock and the marshes beneath, and out over the sea beyond, without wishing that he might have been abbot of that noble Benedictine foundation when it was at the height of its glory. Could he have been that abbot he would have been able to say "religion" as he cannot now say it. For the Mount had, in Henry Adams' words:

> The grand style; it expressed the unity of Church and State, God and Man, Peace and War, Life and Death, Good and Bad; it solved the whole problem of the universe. The priest and soldier were both at home there . . . the politician was not outside it; the sinner was made welcome; the poet was made happy in his own spirit. . . . God reconciles all. One looks back on it as a picture; a symbol of unity; an assertion of God and man in a bolder, stronger, closer union than was ever expressed in other art.*

That experience, at least in those forms, was de-

* Henry Adams, *Mont-St.-Michel and Chartres*, The Massachusetts Historical Society. pp. 44, 45.

nied us with the passing of the Middle Ages, and any attempt to imitate the accent of those days is immediately identified as an ecclesiastical affectation. When modern churches try, after the manner of Mont-Saint-Michel, to become militant on earth, they only succeed in being meddlesome political lobbies. We can no longer speak the word "religion" with the imperial accent that was given it when abbots and kings, monks and crusaders, sat down in the refectory or knelt in the church on Michael's Mount.

In the hope that he may serve us better than the ecclesiastic, we turn to the authentic saint, who vindicates the single-mindedness of true religion, for in his usage all the rest of the vocabulary pays homage to our one word. Here, however, we are met at once by a baffling fact; the saint, so far from making habitual use of the word "religion," speaks it seldom or not at all. The reason for his silence is clear. This word shrouds a high transaction, man's communion with God, and its presence in speech serves to intimate that experience rather than to impart it. The term hangs like a cloud around high altitudes of life and the level world of mundane affairs "wots not what is become" of the saint who enters this "cloud of unknowing." Yet the man who has himself passed into and through this cloud line apparently has little further use for the term itself, since he is in the

34

immediate presence of the realities which the word is intended to suggest.

Thus, no truly religious man, in those moments of his life which give him a right to be so called, ever thinks of himself as "having a religious experience." He does not peek through his folded hands at himself at prayer; he looks into the face of God and gives thanks that his life is preserved. The slightest suggestion of any furtive glancing at himself as being involved in a religious experience invalidates instantly any claim that he may lay to the experience. The saint never says, "I am now having a religious experience." He says, "My Lord and my God." There are in our literature few utterances more religious than Pascal's flaming bit of autobiography, which in its holy urgency does not delay to talk about religion:

This year of Grace, 1654,
Monday, November 23rd,

From about half past ten at night, to
about half after midnight,
Fire.
God of Abraham, God of Isaac, God of Jacob,
Not of the philosophers and the wise.
Security, security. Feeling, joy, peace.
God of Jesus Christ,
Deum meum et Deum vestrum.

The Bible is the most religious book we have, yet
in this indubitably religious book the word "religion"
is almost wholly wanting. It occurs only two or three
times and then merely to indicate the formal practice,
not the inward experience. The baffling absence of
this word from the Bible is not to be laid at the door
of any translator, since the idea itself, in the forms in
which we now employ it, is not present to require
the word or any available synonym. The truth is
that the Bible is much too religious a book to concern
itself with detached talk about religion. The Bible
is a dialogue between God and man, not a reflective
analysis of the situation which requires the dialogue.
The great biblical commandment is not, "Discuss
religious experience," or even, "Get religion"; the
great commandment is much more direct than all
that.

An analogy may be suggestive at this point. The
human experience of love is often employed to intimate the nature of religion. The attitude of the
saint and of the Bible toward religion is that of the
members of some healthy family toward the principle which unites them in a home. In such a human
society the word "love" is not much spoken, nor is it
the theme for constant private self-examination or
common discussion. Presupposing their love for each
other as the nexus between them all, the members
of the home show their love for each other by direct

and constant acts of affection. There is nothing that kills love between us so surely as too much talk about it; perpetual searching into its nature and operations seems to impair its vitality. Nor will "being in love with love" do duty for the immediate and imperious experience itself. The love of men and women for each other is an absorbing passion and refuses to be diverted or delayed by incessant analysis of its processes. Information as to the physiology and psychology of sex is not to be identified with love itself and confusion at this point is costing our time much of its normal human happiness.

This analogy will bear whatever weight of argument we may by inference lay upon it. We often assume that the present widespread interest in religion is a reassuring sign of these times, yet it is a fair question whether our interminable discussions of religion are not the occasion for a profound disquiet. People talk frantically about love not when they are falling in love, but when they are falling out of love. May it be that our time talks so much about religion for the very reason that it has so little religion? Plainly, no decent human home could stand for a fortnight the volume of talk about love, which in another terminology goes on so drearily in our churches about religion. A home driven to that last resort would soon dissolve in laughter or in tears and would end in the mad-house or the divorce court. It is very hard to see why we should go on using in church a type of word which in its parallels in the other vital experiences of life is better left unsaid.

Our present position in this matter was cruelly revealed in a headline of an American daily paper which was reporting not long since the recent missionary congress in Jerusalem: "Mission Leaders Will Discuss Problem of Christianity in Garden of Gethsemane as Jesus Did." The pity of those words lies not so much in the unconscious half-blasphemy of the reporter as in the state of mind to which they were addressed. Plainly, the reporter had served his time on Sunday church assignments and had learned his lesson only too well. His whole contact with churches indicated that when Christians meet together they do so "to discuss the problem of religion." We cannot blame him for assuming that this is the substance of prayer and praise, since he has plainly been at our school and sat attentively at our feet.

America has a pathetic faith in its own swiftly changing slang. Once we were not ashamed to go to a prayer-meeting or to belong to a Bible class, but since these ecclesiastical models are now out of date, we propose in their stead "the religious discussion group." Of all the devices which ingenuity has ever fabricated to stir the spiritual life, this is plainly the worst. It assumes that you can learn about religion from the outside, that you can know the truth without doing the will. The moment its liberal surface is scratched it reveals the hidden apologetic motive; we are trying to save religion by talking about it, one of the most desperate expedients to which organized Christianity has ever been reduced.

We shall get no further with this matter until we realize that talking about religion is not the same thing as finding a way for religion to do its own talking. To discuss religion at arm's length is to make straight for spiritual unreality. The trouble is that it is so easy to talk about religion and so difficult to win a religion that must do its own talking. Being slothful, we choose the easier way.

Our generation is accustomed to blame the elder generation because it offered men a dead theology rather than a living religion, a stone for bread. At this distance we can see the distinction quite clearly. Readers of Gosse's *Father and Son* understand that the younger Gosse was given much highly elaborated Calvinistic talk about Christianity, instead of the Christian religion, and their sympathy is with the lad in his revolt. For, plainly, that sophisticated talk about religion had little of the heart of the living experience left in it. Yet are we in any better position today? We are still busily talking about religion, while we shirk the harder discipline of finding a way for religion to do its own talking. We are superbly accurate in our descriptions of religion— historical, psychological, sociological—and these newer descriptions have plainly found the range more closely than had the elder Calvinism. They are also much more interesting, since they are primarily descriptions of ourselves and we never tire of talking about ourselves; nevertheless they remain descriptions without power to communicate the experience which they describe.

In some ways the present situation is even worse than that which it has supplanted because the sciences of man, and in particular psychology, make constant and facile use of the most intense language of personal piety as their subject matter. A psychological account of a mystical religious experience is so very near the reality, and yet may be so infinitely remote from it. "Oh, the little more, and how much it is! And the little less, and what worlds away!" The body of living religion never seems so alien a fact as when stretched out on the operating table and opened up to be described. The theological uses to which the sciences of man are now put has encouraged a spurious religiosity among us that can deceive the very elect. It is, however, one thing to describe mysticism and another and much harder thing to be a mystic. We are today in grave danger of leaping to the conclusion that persons who can give accurate accounts of religion are religious persons. This, however, is merely substituting theology for religion, the grave error for which we blame the Calvinist so roundly; yet we have merely slipped back into the slough from which we tried to climb out a generation or so ago. Hence the frequency of the word "religion" in our vocabulary is a disquieting phenomenon, since its prominence in speech seems to vary inversely with its presence in life. The less religious we are the more necessary it becomes to talk about religion.

If we go on to ask why this word bulks so large today we shall probably conclude that we say "religion" so often because we say "God" so seldom. It is not wholly surprising that we do not say "God" more often and more confidently, for the elder doctrines of God are plainly inadequate and at certain points in error. The boundaries of our reliable knowledge of the universe have for the moment outrun the limits to which the devout imagination of yesterday had carried our faith. We hesitate to say "God" too thoughtlessly because we are not clear just what we mean or all that we may mean by that word. For this reason we fall back upon the more intelligible word "religion," which does relief duty for the more problematical word "God."

This, however, is only an emergency measure, since religion ultimately stands or falls by its doctrine of God, and the access to God sanctioned by that doctrine. To talk about religion because we are too puzzled to speak to God is merely to postpone our day of religious reckoning. A domestic concern for affairs "human-all-too-human," even in the high name of religion, will not permanently suffice and the apologetic desire to save religion by making it the center of our intellectual interest is not enough. Liberal apologetics in behalf of the validity and worth of religious experience remains apologetics still.

I was much struck not long since by the chance remark of a friend, who has just resigned a chair of apologetics, to the effect that the Christian religion would probably be greatly profited if we all stopped discussing it for a period of ten years. He thought that during such a moratorium our religion might have a chance to recover itself and learn how to do its own talking. A similar statement might well be made about religion in general. Yet one has only to suggest retiring the word from circulation to realize how dependent we are upon it and how difficult it would be to exchange ideas on these matters in want of it. If we should suppress it for a while we should break the wiring between modern minds, we should withdraw from circulation the commonest coin for the exchange of our ideas. Just reader, I make no profession of standing quit of this condemnation. I have realized how hard put to it I should be to communicate with you if I were prohibited from saying, "religion." Yet it seems increasingly clear that this word, with its descriptive concerns, is in danger of getting between us and the realities which at the best it can only intimate. We cannot warm our souls and light our world indefinitely with the stored-up energy of the word "religion"; we must seek sooner or later the Lord and Giver of Light. The habitual use of this word betrays a cloistered virtue and there lingers about it a certain "agoraphobia," a fear of the open places of the universe, the residual timidity of the apologist.

As a friend has it, "If we ever get into heaven it will not be on the strength of any religion that we have identified in ourselves, but of some religion of which we have never suspected ourselves."

CHAPTER THREE

The Truth of the "Cross-Roads"

————————————‹‹››————————————

Some twenty years ago Father George Tyrrell wrote a book called *Christianity at the Cross-Roads*. He was at that time a lonely figure standing at a parting of the ways, not knowing where to turn. He said of himself with wry humor that he had not decided what he would do in the event of the Roman Church leaving him!

The substance of the book never found great favor, but its title caught the common fancy and has now become a platitude. If the apologist leaves his cover and comes out into the open he will find himself being hustled along by a multitude which is keeping holy day at the cross-roads, for since Tyrrell stood there alone and named the place, it has been well advertised and is now badly overcrowded. Most of us have found ourselves there already, and those who suspect that they may not have arrived hurry forward to add to the confusion.

The resulting stir has become so considerable that not only our religion, but most of our other serious interests as well, are adjudged badly in arrears if they are not standing at this congested spot. My *Harvard University Gazette* for the week in which I am writing announces a lecture by a well-known philosopher on "The Theory of Knowledge at the Cross-Roads." The bewildered religionist is not alone and is entitled to the comfort to be had from much distinguished company.

We have been by this time so well advised of the fact of the cross-roads and of the perplexities awaiting us there that there is little help to be had from further warnings. But matters there have come to such a standstill that we shall be greatly indebted to any clear-headed traffic officer who knows how to untangle this jam of institutions, ideas, and duties, and to set us on our way again. What is happening at this much-heralded cross-roads and are matters there as bad as is reported?

Given Father Tyrrell's hard experience, no one questions the propriety of the metaphor as the title for his book. Yet the meaning which was clear to him when he coined the term has been worn off with much handling, and its denomination is no longer certain. What then do we mean when we say that Christianity stands at the cross-roads? If we mean that Christians must try to choose between truth and error, right and wrong, there is nothing new in that;

Christians have always had to make such decisions every mile of their long journey down the centuries. If we mean that we cannot see clearly into the future, and that the future seems to hold many occasions for sober apprehension, again this is not a fresh predicament; no man has ever known what tomorrow might bring forth.

Since the war the phrase has taken on new meanings. Many persons feel that our time was betrayed or self-deceived, and that in an hour of excitement we gave the sanctions of our religion to ventures with which that religion has little or nothing to do. They think that we took a wrong moral turning in history; the journey back has been tedious and humiliating; they propose that another time we shall not be so easily diverted from the main highway of religion. Considerations such as these give a sober content to the metaphor in question.

It is the professional alarmist who is exploiting and abusing this otherwise serviceable figure of speech. His raucous cries about the cross-roads are varied with much like talk of the declines, the collapses, the crises which form his stock in trade. So far as our America is concerned this language tickles a jaded palate that must feed upon exaggeration. The power of understatement is a lost art with us, and chronic overstatement clogs our commerce and vitiates our public life. So far from protecting religion against these rhetorical excesses, we invite them to traffic in our churches as well. Apparently we must provide news of some sort to get a hearing, and if not evangelical good news, then the news so dear to yellow journalism. Our culture, or our want of culture, being what it is, no religious news is as good news as the bad news of the professional alarmist. Plainly the one way to make religion an immediate success is to declare that it is on the verge of imminent failure.

This language of ecclesiastical alarm has made our religion thoroughly valetudinarian. There have been past generations which took their duties to God and man more seriously than we take ours, but there never was a generation that took its "religion" as seriously as we take ours. Religion is compounded of thoughts, feelings, choices which have to do with God and the neighbor. We ourselves slip into the picture unconsciously and eventually find ourselves because we have already lost ourselves in God and in other men. The modern religionist, however, has reversed the process; he spends far too little time praying to God and helping men, and far too much time thinking about his own spiritual condition. This constant taking of our spiritual pulse and temperature, suggested by the alarmist reports that are abroad, is the gravest of all our religious ills.

There is a familiar hymn which, in two of its lines, asks for

> A heart at leisure from itself
> To soothe and sympathize.

Most of what is wrong with modern Christianity is covered by that couplet. We lack any large leisure from ourselves to give to the main offices of prayer and work. If our minds dwelt habitually upon the wonders that are around us and the human wants that are hard by us, rather than upon our own state of spiritual health, we should think much better of Christianity than we now think. For the Christian religion is not intended to be of any help to persons who are more interested in themselves than in anything else in the whole universe, save as it offers to such persons a way of escape from their unhappy obsession with themselves.

The self-conscious and self-centered temper bred by the language of alarms has not been of any actual help to us. If painstaking inquiries into the nature of our distresses could have saved us, we should have been saved long since. A heavy harvest of reports has now been gathered, a summer of surveys is past, and we are not saved. If it be true that organized Christianity is dying before our eyes it will not be for want of help from those within its ranks who have tried to discover in their own members the nature of this, its last and fatal illness.

We have further to reckon with the type of mind that thrives upon test-cases. Mr. Harold Begbie says that he "remembers once speaking to Dr. Winnington Ingram, Bishop of London, about the Virgin Birth. He told me that he had consulted Charles Gore on this matter and that he agreed with Charles Gore's ruling that if belief in that miracle were abandoned Christianity would perish."

This is the sort of notice which a certain kind of dogmatist delights to serve on the world. Now every man comes at last to some point in personal faith where he arbitrarily draws a line. If I cede this, he says, my religion goes. But it is doubtful whether men have either the right or the duty of settling these matters for others. We can only take Dr. Winnington Ingram and Charles Gore at their word; for them Christianity stands or falls by the Virgin Birth. Their private testimony, however, does not rule out of court the evidence of others who have concluded on the ground of experience that the Christian life is still possible in want of this article of the creed.

Never a year passes but our religion is laid on some such latest rack or thrust into some such ordeal by fire. Has it not been loudly heralded abroad within the last twelve months that the South India

Plan is a crisis for the gospel, that in the dispute over the ethics of birth-control our religion is at the cross-roads, that any slightest modification of the Volstead Act means the end of American Christianity? It becomes increasingly difficult to keep our heads level in the midst of this world of awful apocalypses and in moments of impatience we wish a plague on both their houses. Now each of these matters is important and deserves what good judgment and good conscience we can give it; yet no single one of them, nor all together, have been given the power of the keys.

The study of church history should make us very cautious in proposing test-cases for religion. The record is littered page after page with crises, collapses, cross-roads, and extremities of precisely this nature, which were in their own day magnified out of all proportion to the total religious idea. At various times in the past Christians have been violently agitated by differences of opinion as to details of food and drink, by the uncertain date of festivals, by the casuistic riddle of believers who had committed post-baptismal sins, by the marriage of clergy supposed by tradition to remain celibate, by the disputed rights and duties of women in the church, by departures from traditional Sunday observance, and countless kindred matters. Each in its own day and in its own turn was hailed as so critical as to be finally decisive. Yet in spite of the gloomiest prophecies to the contrary, Christianity seems not to have been appreciably impaired, no matter how things fell out. In many of these instances and at this distance only a trained historian can recover the precise nature of the original dispute, and even he cannot stir beneath the slight scar tissue the pains which once were there. We review these matters, as Matthew Arnold would say, with "a smile of wistful incredulity, as though one spake of life unto the dead."

In so far as men are still rash enough to propose these test-cases to God himself, putting him upon the rack of their own ingenuity and uncertainty, the universe refuses to be thus subject to our inquisition. The better mind of our time will have nothing to do with such magic, since it consents to the wise command, "Thou shalt not tempt the Lord thy God." As for the too human habit of proposing test-cases for our fellow men, if conscience does not prohibit it as an unlawful invasion of the rights of private judgment, then prudence should discourage it as dangerous strategy. That memorable day when little Edmund said his prayers to the chair and waited for the lightning to strike him—since the elder Gosse had assured him that God would smite those who bowed down to wood and stone—and nothing happened, is a sober warning to all proponents of religious test-cases. Test-cases more often cost religion than confirm religion. In short the mind which so relates itself to its divine and human environment is wanting alike in faith and charity. These proposed ordeals are skeptical in their origin, being uniformly conceived by a profound uncertainty rather than a steady faith. Persons who believe deeply do not traffic in test-cases.

There is then no duty laid on any of us to be haled into such courts and be judged by such arbitrary standards. We have, on the contrary, a duty to discourage these practices and to expose them for precisely what they are, the desperate resort of an apologetic which is at its wits' ends. When good men are known to differ in both faith and practice we may not allow fanatics to pledge away the whole future of the Christian religion to the highly uncertain issue of controversies over details of doctrine, ritual, morals, or common law. Höffding says with much justice of this type of mind which delights in these test-cases, "No one wants to rob the poor man of his ewe lamb—only let him remember that he must not drive it along the highroad unnecessarily and then demand that the traffic should be stopped on its account."

Indeed, as these summons to submit to test-cases continue to be served on us they seem not only in-

creasingly uncharitable, but also increasingly unim-
pressive. As a friend of mine put it, on being
confronted with the latest ultimatum, "If it be true
that the Christian religion stands or falls upon a
matter of that dimension, then it deserves to fall."
We dismiss, therefore, as historically and religiously
irrelevant this further type of agitation at the cross-
roads.

Having cleared the ground thus far, we must
admit, however, that there are some residual perplexities. Plainly religion is passing through a period
of radical change. We propose, then, to explore the
valid occasion for our much-abused metaphor of the
cross-roads.

Every man of us is in some real measure directly
responsible for the spiritual direction which he gives
to his own life. This is not, however, the whole truth
of his religion, for he is also much affected by the
general drift of his age. If he is a thoughtful man
he will try to estimate the effect of this drift upon
the direction which he chooses for himself. So a man
swimming in the water or rowing on its surface may
seem to himself to be making headway, yet with
reference to fixed points on the shore or in the flood
he may be losing ground steadily. At the mouth of
one of our New England rivers there is a tide-rip,
which, in the days before motor-boats was known as

the "Pull 'n' Be Damned." This hard name was given it by generations of tired fishermen who found that, even though they did their best to row against the current, they lost way when it was running full.

There has been in the past and there still is a great deal of well-meant religious effort which, in relation to the nobler movements of the time, can only be described as a pious "pull 'n' be damned." We respect its holy zeal—what Huss called its *sancta simplicitas*—while we deplore its futility. Sincerity, single-mindedness, in the private determination of our life's direction, is not the whole truth of the religious life, and no man is justified in ignoring the truths of the objective world on the ground that he is sincere in so doing. The pathetic figures in history are not uniformly its more tragic figures; they are quite as often its well-meaning but mistaken persons who have wasted their lives in useless opposition to all that was really prophetic in their time.

That river which we mentioned drains a great tidal basin and presents not only an impossible situation when the mid-tide is running hard, but a baffling situation at each turn of the tide. Toward the moment of low tide the surface water is still running out under the impetus of the ebb. When the sea begins to reassert itself it does so well beneath the surface, and even after the level has actually begun to rise there is a current on top still setting down stream. A like paradox occurs at high tide. The lower waters begin to ebb and the level of the river to drop, while the momentum of the flood is still carrying the surface up stream. One is therefore easily deceived as to what is really happening on that river at such times.

This paradox from nature may serve to suggest a truth about our present religious situation. Few of us probably will waste our strength, pulling-to-be-damned against the stronger currents of our day, but many of us may be mistaken as to the true drift of the time if the tide is turning. Superficially we seem to be well down an ebb tide of interest in the conventional forms of traditional religion. Theology is now no longer able to dictate to the natural sciences how they shall do their work and cannot require them to return to its courts to give account of their findings. Churches can no longer exercise direct control over affairs of state and must content themselves with methods of political indirection. Foreign missions have lost the dogmatic self-assurance of a century ago and now face the non-Christian religions in a more conciliatory spirit. Preachers of the old morality are less truculent in thrusting their codes down the throat of the rising generation. The arrogant self-assurance of organized religion has gone;

the average religionist accepts this dropping tide as his fixed circumstance. He does his best to make some headway against it, yet hardly holds his own; he and all his works seem borne along on the ebb.

Conversely, there are many signs that a fresh flood of religious interest has begun to set. This movement is taking place well beneath the surface of all creeds and churches. Yet a kind of cool and reassuring confidence seems to be coming to us from out of the deeps, with intimations of a more spiritual account of the universe than has been conceded by the frank materialism of the last half-century. This turn of the tide, however, cannot be identified by the surface drift of organized religion, which seems still to be setting in the opposite direction.

Now there is at such a moment a stretch of very confused water over the bar where these currents meet. Whatever is floating there has an uncertain destiny. If the last of the ebb finally carries it across the bar and out to sea it is lost to the river on which it has been traveling. If, however, it is caught and held at the bar it is eventually turned back and restored to the river by the gathering flood. Now the transactions of religion in history take place at two levels. On the surface we meet creeds, churches, rituals, orders, and the like—all the formally organized religious experience of men. Beneath the

surface there is a deep unorganized body of experience, consisting of human intuitions and accesses of
revelation coming from the mystery. The movement
of organized religion at the surface is always being
modified by the drift of this unorganized experience
beneath, and when the two currents come into collision it is uncertain how the lower drift will affect
affairs at the surface.

There have been in the past, and there may well
be in the future, forms of institutional religion that
have been carried so far down the ebb of influence
that they are lost to history. No church or theology
has any guaranty of immortality in history and
should not count on such immortality. We may believe that in the economy of the universe the efforts
of righteous and merciful men are not lost, but there
are plainly formal accounts of religion that have no
historical memorial, or at least no historical survival.
A church should always reckon with the possibility
that it may serve its time and pass away.

On the other hand, institutions on the ebb are
sometimes recovered to history by a change in the
whole deeper drift of the times. The Roman Church
in England was steadily losing its hold over the
people during the fourteenth and fifteenth centuries;
men were growing away from it. Then, at a very low
tide in its affairs, it was caught by the current of

nationalism and reaffirmed as the Church of England. That Church has been since then indubitably English, but whether it is Catholic or Protestant even its wisest minds have never known. Yet we have here the case of a religious institution which seemed to have spent its energy and then renewed its strength because fortified and reaffirmed by forces which it did not originate and which it could not control. And this accident of political history, despite many unlovely accompaniments, has been on the whole a gain for the religious life of Christian England.

Whether some such happy issue is in store for other churches that are today well down the ebb of their influence we cannot say. They may be able to avail themselves of some flooding religious concern and to return to new power. Plainly, however, the peculiar interest of the present moment in the history of Christian thought and life lies in the collision and confusion of these currents which we have identified. In so far as we can estimate what is now happening our age may well be as critical for Christianity as any through which it has ever passed.

For we are rewriting our church history on new premises. We used to assume that Christianity had undergone only one radical change during its nineteen hundred years, that of the sixteenth century. A more careful rereading of the record shows this to be a mistaken interpretation of the facts.

The Protestant Reformation had as its secular preface the Renaissance. The Renaissance was in part the recovery of the lost apparatus of the classical world and in equal part the dim prophecy of the modern scientific age. He is a very wise man who can fairly appraise the precise compounding of these two elements in the thought of the fifteenth and sixteenth centuries. At its outset Protestantism was influenced by both these tempers. It found in the Revival of Learning a means for recovering its lost evangelical sources, and it drew upon the nascent science of the time in its bold interpretation of those sources. Luther's biblical criticism was both devout in its spirit and radical in its method, and in the first free exercise of his Protestant judgment he said bold things about the Bible which no one after him dared say again for another three hundred years.

The tragedy of the Reformation was its early loss of faith in the empirical processes of Protestant thought and its quick reversion to external authority. When, by the time of its second generation, the Reformation had been clearly defined, it issued from that definition much more nearly like the Catholicism it had renounced than had at first seemed probable. There were, it is true, differences of emphasis; but the traditional doctrines of God, Christ, man, sin, grace remained much as before. Theologically the Reformation brought a much less radical change in the main doctrines of the Christian religion than Protestant self-assurance has cared to concede. Protestantism was a new orientation, but by no means a new religion.

The two really critical periods in the history of Christian thought come in the earliest and the latest times, during the first and second centuries, and again during the nineteenth and twentieth centuries.

How Christianity negotiated and survived the transition from the year 30 to the year 150 is an almost inscrutable riddle. The disciples whom Jesus left seem to have expected the near end of the present world-age, the speedy return of Christ, and the beginning of his millennial reign as the vindicated Messiah. Whether they were warranted in this hope by any words of his, or whether they imputed this expectation to him we do not know. The substance of this expectation, whether his or theirs, was residual-Jewish, the precise form and fervor of it were newly Christian. As the first apostles and disciples "fell asleep" and time dragged on it became apparent that this hope was to be deferred; the world was going on as it had gone on since immemorial times. Finally and mysteriously there emerges a

Christianity prepared to live aggressively in a world that is to last indefinitely. In thus restating its hope of the second coming of Christ as the doctrine of the Spirit, and in making its adjustment to an indeterminate historical future, the primitive gospel was radically altered. In particular the early indifference of Christians to the intellectual and institutional furniture of the environing world disappeared. That furniture, once deemed irrelevant to religion because marked down for quick destruction, became necessary to the organized life of the church, and the conquest or exploitation of the legacies of Greece and Rome was undertaken with resolute confidence. This process changed the whole character and complexion of the Christian community. Instead of a loosely united group of believers held tentatively together by the impatient hope of Christ's speedy second coming, we find a strongly centralized and consolidated institution prepared to mediate for an indefinite time its monopoly of the divine grace.

Thus, in the realm of religious ideas it is much farther from the first three gospels to the fourth gospel, from Jesus to the Apologists and Irenæus, than it is from these latter to the break up of Calvinism. In that single hundred years Christian thought traveled faster and to a greater distance than over the seventeen hundred years that follow. How the gospel crossed that high divide between the first apocalyptic hope and nascent Catholicism remains the most interesting and difficult inquiry in Christian history. We would give much to know each step of that way, since we catch so many intimations of its strain and stress.

We thus see in retrospect what the first Christians can have realized only dimly in actual experience, that the years from 30 to 150 were a veritable "crossroads." Whether Christianity took at that time a wrong turning which diverted it from the start, whether we can go back and find the right turning—these are open questions. History has no way as yet of helping us to answer these questions, and such answers as are proposed are prompted by our modern varieties of personal piety, rather than warranted by the imperfect sources. In general, historians incline to conclude that Christianity made with the ancient world the only possible peace, and that this peace was its chance for substantial growth. Be these things as they may, the drastic revision of the substance of the primitive gospel during the first two or three generations was a crisis which makes the subsequent changes of the Protestant Reformation negligible by contrast.

The other critical period in the history of Christian thought is our own time. The issues, which are many and familiar, need not be labored. Plainly, however, the *Origin of Species* published in 1859 was, from the standpoint of traditional Christianity, a far more radical document than the ninety-five theses nailed on the Wittenberg church door in 1517. So also the meeting of the British Association at Oxford in 1860 was, in its implications for the faith, a more signal gathering than the Diet of Worms in 1521. What Luther said to the Emperor Charles at Worms was important, but had been said before by other men, though not perhaps at such dramatic moments; what Huxley said to Bishop Wilberforce was on the whole more important because it had never been said before and was to demand such a drastic revision of the established doctrines of God, man, the process of nature, and the course of history. The period of "restatement" thus begun is by no means ended.

Over the centuries that are gone the Christian religion has had a strange power to possess itself of ideas that were no part of its Galilean heritage, and to turn these ideas to its own account. In particular, from the year 150 through the year 600—*i.e.* from the Apologists through Gregory the Great, Christianity compelled Greek philosophy and Roman law to come and serve it in defining the faith and fashioning the Catholic Church.

During this period, however, our religion was making use of ideas that came ready cut to hand for theological and ecclesiastical uses. This material had already been worked over for centuries with definite reference to the requirements of religion and states-craft, and the great fathers of the church did not have to do their own intellectual and institutional stone-cutting. A wealth of serviceable ideas lay all around the Christian community in the dying classi-cal world, ready to be given a fresh lease of his-torical life when rebuilt into the fabric of Catholic Christianity. It has been said on good architectural authority that there probably was not a single stone used in St. Peter's at Rome which had not been pre-viously a part of some older building. The architects of Christian theology have always been able to work in that way.

Now there is no reason to suppose that this peculiar power of our religion is spent. Christianity may still have the ability to appropriate for its own uses ideas which do not immediately originate with it, provided that they have been worked into shape for the gen-eral intellectual and moral needs of man. The pres-ent problem is, however, a novel one since the newer conceptions of the universe which today are receiving most attention and which seem to hold most promise, come to us as huge uncut blocks from the sources where they are being quarried. Much that we are learning about these matters is, if not religiously re-assuring, at least not prohibitive of religion, but there is one plain fact about it all, this knowledge does not fall naturally into Christian forms. Plato's "Ideas", which the fathers employed to build the Nicene the-ology, were much better adapted to immediate Christian use than are the ideas that occupy the minds of modern physicists and astronomers. These latter considerations are still too rough hewn and unwieldy to be fitted nicely into the delicate window tracery, the flying buttresses, and the fine-spun spires of our cathedral-like systems of religious thought. They might serve as they stand to become the foundations of an entirely new fabric, but they cannot be put under the present building without imperiling its in-tegrity, or used just as they are in repairing the superstructure.

At this point, therefore, history furnishes us no sure and serviceable precedent. Theology has never before been confronted with precisely this situation, and whether it can be resolved by the familiar at-tempt at "restatement" is by no means clear. Even the theory of evolution, which has now been safely domesticated within liberal Christianity, was much more amenable to the methods of conventional Chris-tian apologetics than are these later, more massive and mysterious conceptions now being quarried from "the universe around us." Whether this cosmic stuff will yield to our craftsmanship or will turn the edge of our tools remains to be seen. Hitherto the idea of "personality, human and divine," has been essential to any Christian creed, yet most of this newer body of truth comes to us in patently impersonal forms. It may well be that some giant sculptor can see within these huge blocks an heroic figure, as Michelangelo saw his David in the problematical block of marble which had so long defied the resourcefulness of artists and architects, yet the vindication of personality under such conditions calls for a creative genius which is beyond the powers of the professional apologist. That task demands a prophet, not a scribe.

Perhaps it does not matter whether we allocate this new type of truth, with the certain increment which must steadily accrue to it, to science or religion; what matters is the correspondence of our ideas with reality, the truth of our thinking. If these interpretations of the universe are faithful transcripts of the cosmic fact, they concern us and we must reckon with them. If traditional theology is found to be incompatible with them, then eventually that theology will disappear, since it is not only dangerous, it is impossible, even in the service of traditional faith, to ignore truth. We face, therefore, the possibility that the "local habitations" of religion may not remain indefinitely Byzantine, Romanesque, or Gothic, to say nothing of Georgian and Colonial. It may well be in the realm of contemporary religious ideas, as in the field of architecture, that the discovery of new building material will call for new patterns and designs for its adequate treatment. We should face this prospect with good courage, knowing that in so doing we are still faithful to all that is best and most vital in Christianity.

This novelty of the present situation gives, therefore, a residual measure of sober truth to that metaphor with which we began our chapter and from which we have perhaps strayed too far, "Christianity at the Cross-Roads."

CHAPTER FOUR

The Law of Alternation

————————⟨⟨⟩⟩————————

No living thing has the power to move straight forward in its own element. The environment must provide some purchase for the creature, which gets ahead by a succession of antithetical strokes or thrusts.

In the realm of the arts where man supplements and to some degree corrects nature we may seem to have, as in the case of the moving machine, direct and even motion. This appearance is, however, deceptive and the result is still achieved by employing the principle of alternation in a reciprocating engine or a motor. At the heart of the machine there is the same systole and diastole that we meet in organic life.

This principle seems to be ineradicably imposed upon the whole conduct of life, and conscious art has never freed man from the rhythmical processes of his own nature. So, what we are pleased to call the progress of the race is not achieved along a straight road which climbs directly up the slope; it follows a zigzag trail which leads back and forth on the mountain-side. The way bears to the right until it comes to some insurmountable obstacle or until it bids fair to depart too far from its objective, then by a hairpin turn it doubles back upon itself in the opposite direction.

To use another metaphor, man is a being who has the power to go to windward. The materialistic interpretation of human nature questions this power and requires him to run free before the wind. Yet, materialism to the contrary, nothing is plainer than man's ability to beat into the wind. The spiritual fact is as patent as the nautical fact, however it may puzzle the landlubber. There is only one thing that the sailing-ship cannot do, it cannot go straight to windward; it can, however, point very high into the wind, and by a succession of tacks reach a point directly to windward of that where it started. So the human spirit can point high toward a point which it identifies as "religion"; it cannot, however, make straight for religion; to do so is to come up into the wind, to lose way, to be in irons. For this reason, as we have already indicated, the genuinely religious man never seeks religion as such. What does he seek, then? If he is truly religious he is concerned with two realities—God, and man. This God is a God who is a cosmic being or principle other-than-man. The man with whom he is concerned includes himself, but is by no means confined to himself; he is dealing with what the English mystics of the Middle Ages call our "common human kind." We achieve our religion, therefore, not by addressing ourselves directly to it, but by addressing ourselves to God and man and trying to reach a point where they have something in common. This windward point is what we call religion, and we arrive at it by a succession of long tacks, first in the one direction, then in the other.

Now the whole success of this attempt to get religion depends upon a certain weather wisdom in making the tacks; you have to know when you have sailed far enough in one direction, and when you must come about in the other direction. Our spiritual health and progress consist mainly in striking a fair balance between our two objectives. If the claims of one are pressed so far that we drop the other below the horizon of our interest, what we call "the religious consciousness" flags and dies. Some religions have carried their celebration of the sovereignty of God to such a point that man has ceased to count. Other religions have been so intent to vindicate the worth of man that God can be no longer descried. In such cases either of these would-be religions loses its religiousness, for religion is neither a divine monopoly nor a human monopoly.

Theoretically it ought to be possible to determine at the outset and to maintain thereafter the ideal balance between the two. Perhaps the mystic's moments of perfect peace are proof of such an equipoise, yet by the common consent of all devout souls these moments are rare and very brief. The next item in on-going experience intrudes upon this perfect balance and throws our emphasis in the one direction or the other. Since it is humanly impossible to think of two things at the same time with that single-mindedness which religion requires, our religious life is normally passed thinking first of God and then of man.

The literature of devotion identifies these two contrasted references as the life of prayer and the life of work. There may be a point directly to windward where that motto is true—*Laborare est orare*—yet few of us have ever succeeded in thus identifying these two religious concerns; we have to reckon with them one at a time and in turn. Prayer is man's address to God; work is his concern for this human world. The wisdom of many centuries is constant in saying that we are never well advised to continue too long at one of these vocations in neglect of the other. À Kempis knew that there is a vagabond philanthropy which can be recovered to itself only by the resolute recollection of a soul addressed directly to

God. Saint Theresa knew that there is a point beyond which the vigil of prayer degenerates into sentimentality, and that deliverance from this vice lies in a wholesome concern for the cup of cold water.

As religious persons we often find ourselves at a stage in our history when our religion seems not so much in error as unreal. We cannot reconcile the promise of reality held out by all religions with this increasing sense of the unreality of our own spiritual life. If we take the trouble to consult our situation at such times we usually find that we have been too much concerned for one of the constituent elements of religion and too little concerned for the other. We have sailed so long on one tack that we have run out of the wind. Plainly, when we find that we are passing into these doldrums it is the part of religious common sense to come about and fill away on the other tack. We should all be better Christians if we had a surer instinct when to stop praying and go to work, or when to stop working and turn to prayer. What some one has called "the seeming unreality of the spiritual life" is more often than otherwise this matter of bad proportion.

There is, however, a point beyond which private self-direction in these matters cannot go. If at times we seem to ourselves to be the captains of our souls, at other times we know ourselves to be members of a ship's crew, involved in the fortunes of the vessel and its company. This ship on which we sail is on a long voyage, and that voyage has been for the most part a dead beat to windward. At any particular moment the ship is on a given tack, but it may not have been always sailing in the present direction; indeed, since its course is a dead beat to windward, it must sail on the other tack half the time. Given a historic religion, it is thus at one moment bent upon glorifying God and at another moment upon vindicating man. We might call these two directions, which religion takes in history, its starboard and port tacks. Now if you were born aboard the ship and came to an awareness of yourself as a member of the crew at a time when, in the name of religion, the ship was on the port tack, that must seem to you the normal direction for religion to take. You become accustomed to seeing the sails filled as they now draw, you adjust yourself to the angle of the deck beneath your feet, you stow the gear of your cabin with reference to that list. It is hard for you to realize that there may be another direction required by religion, and if the ship comes about and fills away on the starboard tack your little world will be so altered in its aspects and angles that you will doubt whether this can be religion at all. You naturally assume that religion is to be reached by keeping on in the direction in which you have been taught to expect its realization.

It is only after some personal experience in these matters, particularly after lying for a long time in a dead calm, that you begin to suspect that religion may require of you a reference just the opposite of the one which you have been making. This does not mean that you count your present effort wasted, rather that further progress in religion becomes possible only by changing your course.

In past times the mind of any given age seems to have moved in one or the other, but not in both of these directions, like a single great ship beating up the wind. Today, however, the human mind is divided into two crews that man both types of interest. We are, in Eucken's phrase, "torn by contradictions" to a degree hitherto unknown. The major contradiction of modern thought is that between the objective mind and the subjective mind. The former is intent upon discovering the truth of the outer world, irrespective of any human uses to which that truth may be turned; the latter is bent upon knowing human nature thoroughly and bettering human conditions as rapidly as possible. Neither of these minds, when about its daily business, makes habitual use of the language of theology, yet each of these minds is engaged ultimately on a religious quest, since the findings of both are relevant to any adequate modern religion. The fact that we have these two types of mind at work at the same time need not disturb us; there is indeed much cause for reassurance in this situation, since both are necessary to religion. What troubles us is their failure to understand each other.

The objective mind is reaching out into the remotest mysteries of time and space; the subjective mind is pointing high toward Utopian hopes for man's future. The zest of each of these endeavors is such that neither inquirer can be expected to have a leisurely and sympathetic understanding of the other. Thus, if you are engaged in measuring the remoter reaches of stellar space or finding the pattern of the dance of the electrons, wars and rumors of wars must be left to care for themselves; on the other hand, if you are bent on getting rid of poverty, disease, and unemployment you have no margins of time and interest for the elusive mysteries at the center and circumference of the universe. Plainly there never was an age before our own when as many persons were thinking with such precision and to such good purpose in both these directions. Most of the zest and much of the promise of modern thought lie in this basic contradiction. The only difficulty, from the religious standpoint, is the indifference of these two minds to each other, carried at times to the point of mutual suspicion.

Since religion requires both objective and subjective thinking, it is worth while to allow each proponent to state his own case. We shall find no better witness to the subjective mind than a bold passage in Coleridge's *Ode; Dejection*. The words were written a century and a quarter ago, yet they remain a classic statement of the position. Coleridge is here the pure romanticist. He confesses that there was once a time when he felt the indubitable reality of the outer world, but says that the capacity for such feeling has ebbed and now is lost. True, he can still see the world around, but only as a mirror which reflects himself; the outer order of things is of value to him merely as he can discover in it or can impute to it his own thoughts and feelings. So he looks at the clouds, the hills, and the sea, to say:

I see them all so excellently fair,
I see, not feel, how beautiful they are;

I may not hope from outward forms to win
The passion and the life whose fountains are within.

We receive but what we give,
And in our life alone does nature live;
Ours is her wedding garment, ours her shroud!
And would we aught behold, of higher worth,

Than that inanimate cold world allowed
To the poor loveless ever-anxious crowd,
   Ah! from the soul itself must issue forth
A light, a glory, a fair luminous cloud
   Enveloping the Earth—
And from the soul itself there must be sent
   A sweet and potent voice, of its own birth,
Of all sweet sounds the life and element!

   We in ourselves rejoice
And thence flows all that charms or ear or sight,
   All melodies the echo of that voice,
   All colours a suffusion from that light.

The sort of thing which Coleridge says here so nobly and so unequivocally has been said in a thousand permutations and combinations by the writers of the last century. Indeed, one half of the witness of that century to itself is nothing but an elaboration of this subjective plain-song of early romanticism.

The situation with which we are here dealing is perfectly intelligible. The human spirit is agnostic or skeptical as to the existence in the universe of any reality of equal value with itself. This doubt is not an act of willful ignorance or deliberate arrogance; it is a sober judgment of fact. Romanticism entered the world a century or more ago as the high confidence of the human spirit in its own innate dignity and worth. Man is the measure of all things, and measuring the world of environing nature by himself he is prepared to declare himself potentially, if not actually, the most real fact there is. The world around remains of casual interest, in so far as human emotions can be imputed to it or as human associations cling to it and give it a spurious vitality of its own; otherwise that world seems to be cold, aloof, meaningless, and without independent reality of its own. The thing-in-itself is dead, at least for us. From this type of thought has flowed most of the art, many of the reforms, and much of the religion of the last hundred years.

On the other hand, the development of the natural sciences has produced the opposite type of mind as well, and objective thinking reached by the end of the century a high degree of perfection. The pure scientist begins his inquiries with a determination to rid his thought of the pathetic fallacy which to his mind vitiates romanticism. It is his sober conviction that the uncensored play of subjectivity renders all accurate observation of the natural world impossible. He would therefore purge himself of those too human preferences and passions which incline us to read nature as the reflection of ourselves; he would achieve an unclouded vision of "things-in-themselves." He is not deterred in this endeavor by the truism that all knowledge is in some measure conditioned by the knower, and he will at least begin his search for objective truth by deliberate acts of intellectual and moral self-discipline.

One could quote chapter and verse to the point of tedium in illustration of this aspect of all first-rate scientific thinking. Huxley says that we must sit down before facts as a little child, give up every preconceived idea, follow wherever and to whatever abysses nature leads or we shall learn nothing; that way only lies peace of mind. Huxley had learned this lesson from Charles Darwin, who says of himself that he always made a special point of noting those facts which told against his theories rather than those which told for them, since we are so inclined to grasp at that which bears out our preference. To this constant habit of marking exceptions and never letting them pass unnoticed he says that he owes whatever success he had as a scientific thinker. Faraday says that the mind of the scientist is littered with theories that have been crushed in silence and secrecy by his own criticism and self-examination. Theodore Richards, who received at the end of his life the Nobel prize for his researches in chemistry, counsels us to purge ourselves of the very human tendency to look only at the favorable aspects of our work and to be ever on the lookout for self-deception; each mental step we take is to be questioned.

Citations to this same unvarying effect might be multiplied at will; they form the morality of all those who work in the pure sciences. The ideal is that of a mind rid in so far as is possible of all human passion and preference. The romantic mind may decree its pleasure domes in Xanadu, but the scientific mind has not the slightest interest in those decrees or confidence in their efficacy. It elects to look steadily at the outer world with which, rightly or wrongly, it tries to deal as being at least of equal reality with itself. "The facts that Science takes to do with," says Sir J. A. Thomson, "are 'real,' and 'what is real means something which we do not make, but find.'" Romanticists may make and remake worlds to their hearts' content, pure science deals with a world order which it finds already in existence and its one aim is to "vibrate in unison with that order," to understand it by making a working thought-model of it. Pure science has a profound distrust of romanticism and much prefers its meager fifty years of realism beneath a telescope or over a microscope to the dreamy cycles of a highly subjective Cathay.

Now the gravest difficulty which religion encounters in our time has its origin in the failure of these two sharply differentiated types of mind to understand and to allow for each other. The man who takes a frankly interested and subjective view of things is chronically impatient with the occupations of the pure scientist, which, to his thinking and in Novalis' phrase, "bake no bread." He doubts all talk of a truly disinterested inquiry into truth and suspects it of being a veil for some disguised selfishness. He is eager to get on with the human job and has a constitutional aversion to those who will not sign on for his reforms and crusades. He inclines to dismiss pure science as pure snobbishness or pure pedantry. In short, he simply cannot envisage a life spent in a laboratory trying to find out what is so, without any consideration of the human account to which the findings may be turned. He cannot understand why men go to the Poles or try to climb the Himalayas when there is nothing useful there to bring back.

Conversely, the pure scientist is apt to look upon his romantic contemporary with a certain patrician tolerance. He agrees with Thoreau that many of our reforms are "an improved means to an unimproved end." His mind is accustomed to press on to very remote conclusions and he knows why Tyrrell said, "When everybody is properly clothed, housed, and fed the question still remains what to do with life, a question to which they have no answer for whom philanthropy is the whole of religion." He does not demand that people shall go naked and hungry, but he does insist that creature contentment is not the whole of life; he demands that we shall glorify and enjoy our universe. He believes that to know is itself a worthy end in life and he adds the years of his toil to his initial faith.

He realizes also that the too calculating eye, squinted at human profit and loss, costs men their vision of the truth. He has learned that the relationship is a moral one, and that he will find the truth only as he seeks it for its own sake. Did we not overhear Theodore Richards saying to a group of theological students that as a professional chemist he was interested only in the chemical structure and properties of TNT and had no concern with the uses to which it might eventually be put—whether to clear stumps in a forest to make place for a squatter's farm, or to blow up Germans in a trench to make the world safe for democracy? There was an unspoiled human being at the core of Theodore Richards, who still cared for these matters, but he was on the only sure ground tenable by pure science when he held to his original contention. His first and only task as a research chemist was to determine this combination of elements and its properties.

Now these two types of the modern mind are not new; they are, in fact, very old. Religion has been familiar with them for centuries, since they are the contemporary manifestations of the two persistent strains which we identify in the history of religion as magic and mysticism.

The romantic and subjective mind of today, particularly in its humanitarian guise, would be the first to repudiate the charge that it was magical in intention. Yet in so far as magic rereads nature in the terms of human interests and tries to get nature on man's side by cajolery or coercion, there is in much of the humanitarian thinking of the day a strain of residual magic. If we conclude that we are the realest objects in the universe, it is both our right and our duty to take ourselves seriously and make the rest of the universe help us realize our desires. I will try to climb Mount Everest or trudge to the North Pole if it can be shown that these adventures are of any human use or that men will profit thereby. But if I am a pure romanticist and humanitarian I certainly will not go just for the fun of it, or for the sake of seeing what it is like when I get there. This fixed mental habit of the subjectively conditioned mind to measure the rest of the universe by itself puts it in the magical succession. It is true that the ends envisaged by that mind, in its genial modern incarnations, are ethically much more laudable than those proposed by primitive magic. Thus, religion which was once a help in making war shall now be a help in making peace, yet the peace as well as the war is something we wish for ourselves and without which we cannot get along. The League of Nations is a distinct improvement on the wars of the nations, but its reference is still directly human; we must have it or something like it because we cannot afford to run the risk of being longer without it. The technical coercive apparatus of primitive magic has been abandoned, the ends which we propose have been purified and elevated, yet the general reference of magical religion remains; we do these things because they contribute to our welfare and happiness; therefore we demand a God whom we can use.

The pure scientist, on the other hand, is the heir of much that in the past we have identified as mysticism. His disinterested concern to know what is so is very like the selflessness which the mystics have always preached. I have long thought that there is probably far more genuine mysticism in the research laboratories of our universities and great industries than is to be found in psychological class-rooms where we study mysticism or in sentimental religious groups where we play at being mystics. In pure science we have the authentic mental and moral transaction in its realistic contemporary form. The disinterested search for truth is one of the finest manifestations that the mystical temperament has ever known. Darwin, Faraday, Huxley, Theodore Richards need concede nothing to the author of the *Theologia Germanica* with his doctrine of the unmercenary love of God. What they have to say about eradicating the stubborn, "I, Me, Mine, and the like" runs true to form. And when Faraday says of the scientist in the passage already cited, that "his nature must be one which vibrates in unison with that of which he is in search," he is using words which would be in place in any manual of classical mysticism. The intellectual effort to discipline your thought so that it shall accord perfectly with what is so is utterly void of the magical reference and can be classified only under this other religious category. It is my own conviction that few men in our modern world live more single-minded and truly mystical lives than do the best of our scientists. I can conceive of no adequate modern religion which does not include them in its scope, and require their contribution to the realization of its ends. Their humility and reverence shame the candidly interested religion of many conventional "rice Christians." They need have no fear that they cannot face the Wisdom and Spirit of the Universe with a good conscience. For they have never sought to exploit for trivial and ephemeral ends the great realities to which their minds are steadily addressed.

Here we have, then, these two types of mind in our world today: a generous and hopeful humanitarianism which as a racial effort states religion subjectively, a scientific dispassionateness which, in so far as it envisages religion, thinks objectively. Never before have men thought and toiled so hard and in such numbers to realize these two legitimate ends. More persons care today than have ever cared before, on the one hand to know what is so for the sake of knowing, and on the other hand to make this world a better place for man to live in. These enterprises are being carried on in part with the help of churches, theologies, and creeds; and in equal part without that help. Since thought is intense and effort genuine in each of these areas, here is the crude stuff of experience from which a new religion may be fashioned, or with which the religion that is old must reckon.

The problem of the moment is how to get and keep these two types of mind in some direct relation, so that each shall fulfill the other. The difficulty is that no one man, under present conditions, can do both things effectively. As life is now organized you ought not to take the chemist away from his laboratory for six months out of every year and require him to serve on a committee to relieve unemployment. Nor can you draw off some member of the secretariat at Geneva, who is busy with delicate political negotiations, and put him to work in an observatory counting stars. Religion has no right to waste men's lives by diverting them from tasks at which they are supremely efficient and setting them to do jobs at which they would be ineffectual. We do not require a Coleridge to stop writing poetry and turn to breeding pouter pigeons, or a Darwin to give up breeding pouter pigeons and start dreaming of ancient mariners and pleasure domes—all for the sake of some more systematic and perhaps sophisticated account of what religion is. Each of these men, in the name of religion, must be encouraged to get on with his work; for there lies his chance of making a genuinely religious contribution to the thought and life of his time.

But those of us who are neither great poets nor pure scientists should make a point of having friends in both camps. Our present danger is that, having too many friends in one camp, or trusting too much to our amateur sympathies in this direction or that, our account of religion may be so one-sided as to become eventually irreligious. Every one of us needs correction at this point, toward a greater subjectivity or a greater objectivity of interest. The apologetic business of fitting random items of late truth into the conventional mosaic of traditional theology is a very dull occupation beside the exciting task of trying to prophesy the revival of religion which may follow if we can get these two types of mind well introduced to each other and require them to compound or equate their dual interest fairly. When the moral law within and the starry heavens above lose all touch with each other, religion dies. The maturity of "the mind of Christ" is the ability to envisage both at the same time and to affirm them as the two shields of one reality.

In so far as the present age is critical for religion it is critical then, not merely for the reasons indicated at the end of the last chapter, but for this further reason as well—and the words are Eucken's—"Our time remains painfully wavering between the absorption of the subject by a too powerful object, and the dissipation of the object by a too self-sufficient subject." Many of the old dogmas of orthodox theology are plainly passing away before our eyes. That is a minor matter; theologies ought to change and pass. This is not that "decay" or "decline" of religion about which we hear so much. If it be true that we men of today are somehow less capable of being religious than our predecessors were, we must attribute that liability to the fact that the subjective and the objective types of mind misunderstand and mistrust each other to such an extent. You cannot have religion when these two minds fall out with one another. You must insist that the Coleridges and the Darwins shall not go on doing their work in ignorance and neglect of each other. Their willingness to recognize each other and their maturing ability to understand each other are the very subsoil and premise of whatever varieties of religious faith and practice may follow.

The falling out of these two types of mind must inevitably mean a decay of religion, and there is no doubt that in this respect our present religious difficulties are very considerable. Conventional apologetics can be of little help here, since neither the Coleridges nor the Darwins are apt to be well known to the apologist; therefore he will be at a loss how to introduce them to each other and get them to talking together. That is, however, the religious task of the hour.

CHAPTER FIVE

Whence Liberalism?

———————————‹‹››———————————

Just after the war John Morley published his *Recollections*. A strain of regret runs through this gracious autobiography at the passing of that liberalism with which he had been so long identified. The war found him an old man and it was too late for him to grapple with an age driven by forces which he could neither understand nor arrest. "The world is travelling fast under formidable omens into a new era, very unlike the times in which my lot was cast."

The disappearance of the liberal from the political scene, even though this eclipse be only temporary, is one of the striking facts of the day. The liberal is not puzzled by his present lack of power, for how can he expect to influence a time which has either reverted to conservatism or rushed into radicalism; but he is sobered by his present lack of opportunity. At the moment there does not seem to be anything for him to say or do; he is a man without a country.

Now the liberal, whatever his other defects, had this excellence, he had unified his life to a very high degree. He may have been ineffectual at times; he was never hypocritical, since he had put away those departmental theories of life which make for hypocrisy. He was not uniformly a churchman, yet he always had a sympathetic interest in religion, and such religion as he had was a part of the whole man. Since he never tried to separate his religion from the rest of his life, that religion cannot remain immune to his change of political fortune, and he finds himself wondering whether this change must affect his religious fortunes adversely. Will he have to turn his once genial faith into a city of refuge where his hopes, temporarily thwarted in the wider world, may take shelter? Will his churches, he asks with wry humor, become what the monasteries were to the Dark Ages, fortresses to keep alive the gracious wisdom of the past against some better future?

The remainder of these pages are addressed to those who for the want of any better designation call themselves liberals in religion. This word has become a blanket term to cover all persons who no longer subscribe to the full creed of·traditional orthodoxy. Who are we? Where did we come from? How have we come to be what we are? Where are we going? What is to become of our cause? We are by no means clear about our present and future, we only know that we cannot turn traitors to our liberalism and make our submission to Catholicism, Fundamentalism, and the like.

The word "liberalism" is very loosely used in modern religion. More often than otherwise it is employed to label that particular type of thought which dispenses with all creeds and allows entire liberty of private opinion. An Anglican convert to Rome once said that he could see in the Church of England merely a body of people bound together by a prayer-book and an agreement to differ on every important point of doctrine. If this account of the case is correct, then the Church of England is a liberal church, for liberal churches assume that their members need not agree in matters of faith and conduct. Strictly speaking, however, this is a matter of latitudinarianism rather than liberalism, and it is a fair question whether a church which makes its only dogma an absence of all dogma ought to be called liberal, since the term has a clear content of its own.

Modern liberalism came into political being as a revolt against monarchies, autocracies, oligarchies, and the like. We know it best as the outworking of the forces that led to the French Revolution. It has two at least of its classic statements in the American Declaration of Independence and the French Declaration of the Rights of Man, which were assertions of the value of the common man as against all usurpers.

Morley states the essence of liberalism in a single phrase, "respect for the dignity and worth of the individual." Wherever we turn in the authentic liberal record we find this brief creed, or its equivalent. Liberalism, then, is not a creedless philosophy for church and state; it has as clear-cut a dogma as any other movement—it is a belief in man.

We are familiar today with the statement that faith in the value of the individual is one of the two or three cardinal doctrines of Christianity. At this distance we cannot tell how much we owe this modern dogma to the teaching of Jesus and how much to Rousseau and his successors. If the idea is plain in the gospels, it is not so plain that Christians have not been able to ignore it for long periods in the past. There is much reason to suppose that this article of our American Christianity derives quite as directly from our political history as from our theological inheritance. Plainly, it would have been much harder for us to believe in the value of the individual had the American Revolution failed, as it would be much harder to hold this faith today were we living in illiberal Russia or illiberal Italy.

Yet it is not a fair reading of the facts to say that liberalism in religion was with us a pious afterthought prompted and warranted by our political history. For liberalism is a phenomenon which tends to recur in religion with reasonable constancy. We cannot predict its appearances and reappearances with the precision that is possible in making an astronomical calculation, but there are conditions periodically reappearing in history that seem to breed liberalism more or less automatically. Religion in history gets on, as we indicated in a previous chapter, by a law of alternation. It addresses itself now to the sovereignty of God and now to the worth and rights of man. When one of these ideas has been carried to its logical conclusion and its resources exhausted, the mind naturally turns in the other direction. In this broad sense of the word liberalism is a recurring phenomenon in the history of religion, which follows those periods when theology overstates its doctrine of God. Apparently man may be relied upon to reassert himself in the name of religion when the idea of divine sovereignty has been carried to excess.

If we review the last three thousand years of consecutive Jewish-Christian tradition we can identify these liberal reactions. The religion of Israel as first formulated conceded little or nothing to the individual. He had no independent dignity and worth, such dignity and worth as he had attached to him through his membership in Jehovah's chosen people. Pre-exilic religion in Israel was objective-minded. With exilic and post-exilic times the occasions for introspection were multiplied and we have a much more subjective account of religion. The God of the later prophets is not so arbitrary as his predecessors; he concedes much more worth and initiative to the single Jew. The moral apparatus for making men individually good is elaborated; interior piety develops and creates its own literature; there are intimations of a doctrine of personal immortality; the sacrifices of the temple are succeeded by the edification of the synagogue.

The gospels are difficult to classify. They are the heir of all the intense private piety which Pharisaism had sought to perfect, and of their tender human solicitude there is no least doubt. Yet the gospels were not humanist tracts for their times, since the whole scene is dominated by the thought of God the Father and his heavenly kingdom. The gospels seem to sum up the earlier objective and the later subjective trends in Jewish thought and to set them in some kind of fair relation. Religion, as Jesus thought of it, is neither a divine monopoly nor a human monopoly, it is a free relation between beings each of whom has a respect for the dignity and worth of the other. They are right, therefore, who find in the gospels the distinctive idea of liberalism, confidence in the value of the individual, but they are wrong if they find only this idea there; the other idea is there as well—God, his Will, his Kingdom.

The gospels seem thus to mark one of those rare moments in the history of religion when the outward-turned mind and the inward-turned mind understood and complemented each other perfectly. This equipoise of religious reference ought to be at least one essential part of what is meant by "the mind of Christ." We have constant occasion to note in the life and words of Jesus the absence of that tension which we usually find in the religious consciousness. We usually describe this want as the lack of any sense of sin in Jesus. We are probably nearer the fact if we say that in the religious thought of Jesus the balance of the rival claims of God and man is for once fairly struck. The words "ancient" and "modern" have little meaning here; the words "mature" and "immature" are much more pertinent. The gospels are ancient books, but they are religiously very mature books, and mere modernity in these matters is no guaranty of maturity, since many modern accounts of religion are at this point hopelessly immature. The mind of Jesus was, so far as we can see, more mature at this vital point than most minds of which we have prior or subsequent record. In our immaturity, our strong predilection for a too objective or a too subjective religion, we still invite the words, "Let that mind be in you which was also in Christ Jesus."

When we pass on into the first Catholic centuries we meet again the outward-turned mind. The great objective fact during those years is the Catholic Church, nascent, emergent, and at last triumphant, which restates in the terms of its own institutional requirements the doctrine of the absolute divine sovereignty. The church overtopped the lives of individual men as the cathedral towers overtopped the roofs of the little houses gathered under its eaves. The whole reference of mediæval Christianity is in the direction of God, his Son, the Virgin Mother, the saints, all in heaven, as these were manifest through the church. As some one has it, "The cathedrals were built at a time when men did beautiful and useless things for the sake of an idea." This is the sort of luxury which liberalism challenges and denies, since such wanton prodigality serves no plain human use and ministers to no immediate human need.

With the advent of the Middle Ages, however, a humanitarian reaction sets in. Lay brotherhoods professing a simple biblical Christianity begin to appear; the Bible is made accessible to the common man in the vernacular; the feudal order is no longer taken for granted; prelatry is under fire; the unclassed and neglected become active in their own behalf. Eventually the Revival of Learning recovers much that was best in the classical humanism of a remote time. The Protestant Reformation which followed was not so much the birth of these various movements which looked to the vindication of the individual, as their consolidation. The Reformers of the sixteenth century were not ploughing a field, they were harvesting a crop which had been sown as early as the thirteenth century and had been maturing for the intervening three hundred years. It is quite as true to say that the Reformation was the end of a period as to say that it was the beginning of a period.

For Protestantism was no sooner promulgated as a declaration of the religious rights of the individual than it lost faith in its own dogma. Luther may have begun his reforming work by assuring his contemporaries that "a Christian man is the most free Lord of all," but before long he had occasion to curb this freedom. Münster was an overstatement of the Protestant case; it was liberalism gone mad. The inference which zealots drew from the new ascription to them of spiritual dignity and worth outran the intention of the more sober Reformers, and we have in the Genevan theocracy a reaction toward a more objective type of religion. The phrases of Calvin's *Institutes* sound out like some great cathedral bell calling men back again from their too human self-confidence to that "sense of Deity inscribed on every heart."

For two hundred years organized Protestantism remained outward-minded, and in Calvinism it elaborated to a degree never before achieved the dogma of the divine religious monopoly. In the Puritanism of the early eighteenth century there is less concession of man's worth and less place for man's initiative in religion than can be found at any other time in Christian history. Man as a free being with a dignity and worth of his own had been crowded out of the picture. God was all in all. If the religion of humanity had run wild at Münster the religion of Deity had lost all sense of proportion in New England. Calvinism ceased then to be a religion and survived only as a theology, hardly that if theology is the science of religion, since later Calvinism is little more than a cosmology and a philosophy of history. This high Calvinism was a magnificent structural system, but it was not a religion, since man counted for nothing in it, save as furnishing God added occasion for increasing his own glory. Using the word in its technical sense, Puritanism was a thoroughgoing illiberal religion.

Now we are well within the facts when we say that even had there been no liberal forces at work in other areas of life during the eighteenth century, a liberal reaction was due and overdue in religion. The illiberal theology of the day was itself sufficient occasion for a protest; man was bound, in the logical course of things, to reassert himself against the Sultanic God who was supposed to determine his destiny so arbitrarily and unjustly. The human conscience had to go on record against such a state of affairs and human nature had to vindicate again its own dignity and worth.

There are clear intimations that such a reaction had already begun in New England prior to and quite apart from imported European ideas about the rights of man. More than one Puritan minister had come about and filled away on the other tack in religion before any rumors of Rousseau came over the sea. The convictions which such men arrived at independently were, it is true, greatly fortified at a later time by the success of the American Revolution, but that Revolution itself was in part made possible by the spread of ideas about human nature which had been first ventured as rank heresies in New England meeting-houses. The ministers in those meeting-houses would not have preached treason to an English sovereign with such good conscience had they not already begun to make good their revolt against an arbitrary divine sovereign.

Those who care to do so may read this story in

some detail in Professor Schneider's *Puritan Mind*.*
A few brief or free citations from his pages must
suffice us here. He identifies the Reverend Samuel
Johnson, born at Guilford, Connecticut, in 1696 as
the father of liberal Christianity in America. Johnson was not a man of any theological parts, but by
the time he was thirty years old he was prepared to
break with his Puritan inheritance and environment.
He was unable to think as meanly of man as current
dogmas required, and coveting a more humane out-
look he crossed to England and took Anglican orders.
He seems to have been a genial gentleman, impatient
of theological sophistication, and he demanded ur-
banity in religion; in particular he was sure that
belief in the absolute sovereignty of God was doing
religion more harm than good. From his many and
in the main unimportant writings,

One spark caught fire; the reassertion of human agency and
freedom. This doctrine became increasingly popular and fed the
growing spirit of liberty. Johnson, of course, meant free-will,
not free thought; and moral responsibility, not political liberty;
but any idea which defended any freedom was welcomed in
those days (as in these) for its liberalism. . . .

His substitution of human happiness for the glory of God as
the chief end of man opened the way for the humanitarian revolt against Puritanism. . . . His ethics is conceived not in the

* Herbert Wallace Schneider, *The Puritan Mind*. Henry Holt &
Company, Inc.

Puritan terms of the glory of God, but in the rationalist terms of happiness; and happiness is defined as the complete realization of all the capacities of the soul. . . . Johnson's God was a humane God. Therefore no offense to the glory of God is committed when man pursues his happiness even in this world. . . . The idea of happiness once admitted, worked like a leaven, until, less than a century later it had overturned the whole system to which Johnson had temporarily reconciled it. Johnson opened the door to human nature, and all that remained to be done was to cancel the eternal part of the soul and eternal happiness, in order to usher in a humanistic, worldly utilitarianism. . . .

At the time Johnson took this step he was conscious that he was dethroning the sense of sin, but he little realized that men would find happiness apart from God. . . . The Puritan world was crumbling. Johnson attempted to escape from its ruins and sought refuge in the urbane culture, orderly government and worldly wisdom of the Anglican Church and the British nation. But this escape proved impossible in New England. The new forces which were impinging upon American society and thought he failed completely to understand. He did not know that liberty was creating a new religion.*

Johnson had a successor in Jonathan Mayhew, minister of the West Church in Boston during the middle of the eighteenth century. Mayhew denied the doctrine of irresistible grace, sought truth in natural religion, supplanted doctrinal preaching by sermons on political matters, and for the glory of God substituted moral and social concepts. He believed

* Op. cit. pp. 183, ff.

that God is concerned above all else to bring us into right relations with our fellows that the sum of human happiness may be thus augmented. By the third quarter of the century Mayhew was preaching political sedition as a religious right and duty. By the end of the century and after the Revolution, Charles Chauncy, Mayhew's colleague and successor, is stating an American truism when he says that "the whole human race are made for happiness."

Such were the beginnings of liberalism in American Christianity. Man is here conceived as a being of native dignity and worth, as capable of moral initiative, as meant for happiness both here and hereafter. This whole type of thought, which had an independent birth within Puritanism, was much fortified by the spread of radical political ideas to the same effect, imported from Europe. It is, however, impossible to dismiss this New England liberalism as a theological aftermath of French republicanism, since it was evoked by the reliable logic of thought operating within the religious tradition in the Colonies.

What emerges from it all, when the dust has cleared away, is Chauncy's unqualified dogma that man is made for happiness, which becomes the first article of the liberal creed. Any attempt to introduce prior articles ignores the actual time process in the

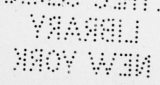

writing of the liberal creed, since that creed began with the statement, "I believe that man was meant to be happy." This article of faith called for a revised doctrine of God, and Chauncy is significant as a religious thinker, not because he repeated what Johnson and Mayhew had said before him, but because he followed the logic of the position common to them all, and substituted the doctrine of the divine benevolence for that of the divine sovereignty. We are in the habit of assuming today that faith in God's goodness and loving care is the first article in the liberal creed. Historically this is not so; that is the second article of the creed, which follows as a necessary corollary from the prior article. The initial conviction as to man's nature and destiny required this account of God to confirm and to guarantee it. Modern liberalism has been constantly embarrassed by the difficulty of deducing its confidence in the goodness of God from the cosmic order, since the facts of this order do not point uniformly in that direction. Our modern faith in God's goodness is historically more intelligible and perhaps theoretically more defensible when we realize that, as first stated by liberalism, it had no connection with the cosmic process, but was a deduction from the particular view of man held by the rebel liberals of the time. Since man is meant for happiness, any God there is must be

concerned to further that end, and the divine benevolence is therefore required by the major premise.
We should not forget, when dealing with liberal
Christian thought, that its doctrine of God is always
conditioned by a prior doctrine of man.

It is not to be supposed that liberalism won an
instant and easy victory in the churches. Bellamy,
Hopkins, Emmons, and Dwight remained uncom-
promising advocates of the sovereignty of God, and
the survival forms of this dogma are still to be identified in the fundamentalist churches. The Congrega-
tional churches which became Unitarian were the first
to give liberal religion institutional standing. The
Unitarian movement is badly misjudged if it is dismissed merely as a denial of the deity of Christ; its
changed Christology was merely a single item in a
much more thoroughgoing restatement of the Christian position. Unitarianism was a consistent affirmation of the whole liberal doctrine of man, and in
so far as other churches have departed from the
Puritan distrust of man, their vindication of man
has been made possible in some very real part by the
pioneer work of the Unitarians of a century ago.

Professor Schneider brings his reflections upon this
chapter of church history to the following close,—

The pursuit of happiness and the exercise of benevolence
were henceforth not merely secular aims of a new nation, they

were embedded in "The Scheme of God," as the essential attributes of Deity. The moral revolution in New England from Puritanism to Americanism transformed God from the Perfect Being of Edwards into the Universal Benevolence of Chauncy. . . .

To use the words of Dr. Gay, "The dispensations of God's providence" were at last "adjusted to the devotions of his people." Like his people God had become devoted to human happiness and to that kindly benevolence "which constitutes us worthy objects of each other's love, and lays the foundation for that mutual trust between man and man, without which there could be no such thing as public happiness." God himself had become republican.*

If there be today any such vague genius as "the religion of America," it is the kind of religion foreshadowed by Johnson, Mayhew, and Chauncy. The average American thinks that man is the sort of person they dared to believe him to be, not the miserable and negligible creature that Puritanism had accused him of being. The daily life of the modern American citizen, with the ends that he proposes to himself in conduct, the morality that determines his choices, the faith that sustains him in adversity, are all characteristically liberal. In the best sense of the word, he believes in himself. No matter what ancient theology he may profess in church, the religion by which he actually lives, earns his daily bread, founds his

* Op. cit. pp. 201-202.

home, raises a family, and at the last passes on the torch to another generation, is that of the sermons of Charles Chauncy and of the preamble to the Declaration of Independence, not that of the *Institutes* of Calvin or the treatises of Jonathan Edwards. The normal American still believes in his right to happiness, and his dignity and worth which warrant that happiness; then adds to this faith his further confidence in some principle in the universe, which in his bolder moments he calls a Father, that sanctions his search for happiness and aids him in this search. Such is the popular and effective religion of America.

Up to the present time at least it has been treason to question this faith, and un-American to say that man is not a creature of the worth and dignity affirmed by the dogma, and that it is uncertain whether his main business in life is to be happy. It is true that orthodox churches, Jewish, Catholic, and Protestant alike, have continued to defend the elder and less reassuring doctrine of man, and that the contrast between orthodox religions on the one hand and orthodox politics on the other hand has created an anomalous situation in America for a century and a half. We wonder that men have not been more acutely uncomfortable at this discrepancy, since the religion which they practise in their lives on the week days, a religion which is consistently liberal, gives the lie to the illiberal creeds which they mechanically recite on Sundays. We can only conclude that the Puritan theology has caused so little discomfort precisely because it is nothing but a theology, and is no part of the religion by which America lives.

That Puritan theology is being slowly disintegrated, not so much by scientific criticism as by the steadily rising level of comfort, the increasing prosperity, the ever wider opportunities of the common citizen. The only conceivable event which might shake this living and operative religion of America is a national catastrophe of such a magnitude as to make us doubt our dignity and worth and inalienable right to happiness. Had the iron of the last war actually entered our vitals we might have doubted our liberalism; as it is we were not badly enough hurt to suffer in our self-assurance, and indeed the post-war happenings have done much to fortify us in our national self-confidence.

If time and space allowed we could linger for an indefinite time following the elaborations of the liberal doctrine in many fields and through many lands, during the nineteenth century. One has, for instance, only to remember the romantic movement in letters to see how all that was best in the literature of the last century and a half was the product of the liberal spirit. Given Wordsworth, Coleridge, Byron, Shelley, Tennyson, and Browning in England; given Franklin, Cooper, Emerson, Thoreau, and Walt Whitman in America; given these and many others like them, it is not hard to understand how liberalism became the dominant faith of the period. For men found that they could still have a religion in want of any belief in the kind of God whom traditional orthodoxy preached, and that this religion had life, color, beauty, and moral power. So Mark Rutherford writes of his experience as a theological student threshing over the barren straw of Calvinism in an orthodox seminary,

One day in my third year, a day which I remember as well as Paul must have remembered afterwards the day on which he went to Damascus, I happened to find amongst a parcel of books a volume of poems in paper boards. It was called *Lyrical Ballads*, and I read first one and then the whole book. It conveyed to me no new doctrine, and yet the change wrought in me could only be compared with that which is said to have been wrought on Paul himself by the divine apparition. . . . It excited a movement and a growth which went on till, by degrees, all the systems which enveloped me like a body gradually decayed from me and fell away into nothing.*

We do not forget what Huxley wrote to Kingsley, "*Sartor Resartus* led me to know that a deep sense

* W. Hale White, *The Autobiography of Mark Rutherford*, T. Fisher Unwin, p. 18.

of religion was compatible with the entire absence of theology." We find Morley acknowledging a similar indebtedness: "Whatever else may be said, it was, I think, at any rate possible to be, or think yourself, a fervent disciple of Ruskin, without adhering to a single article of theological tradition or authority. As much may be said of Carlyle, whom Ruskin called his master."

Such were the men and such were the forces which marked the reaction of that time against the incredible and ungenerous dogmas offered by churches and states in the mid-eighteenth century. Those rebels and prophets of yesterday established us in a noble tradition and have left us immeasurably their debtors. They found us groveling before the universe, and in the name of religion they said, "Son of man, stand upon thy feet." They bred the self-reliance which comes from a true self-knowledge and a proper self-respect. There is no undoing what they have done, no repudiating their works. Even though the greatest figures in this liberal tradition seem to us to belong to the past rather than the present, their works do follow them.

Yet having said so much, we must admit that liberalism is not necessarily a total religious truth. It was historically occasioned and required, it has been historically conditioned, and like all similar ideas it is liable to the fortunes of time. Since the past history of the liberal movement is reasonably intelligible and since the main doctrines of liberalism are now a matter of our second mental nature, we ask whether religion has more to seek and find down this direct road which we have been traveling for the last two hundred years. Does the gleam still lie straight ahead? That is a question to which the answer is by no means clear.

And meanwhile what of the apologist whom we are trying to drive out from his cover? In his orthodox incarnation he does not exist in the liberal churches. We have among us no professional class whose business it is to defend the discarded dogmas of yesterday. We have, however, bred up our own variety of apologist, a man whose task it is to vindicate our kind of religion. Since the premise of liberalism is its genial doctrine of man, the specialized task of defending our faith has been put of necessity into the hands of those persons who study the sciences of man: the historian, the sociologist, the economist, the psychologist—particularly the psychologist. These persons hold, from liberal Christianity, a roving commission to defend religion liberally construed. They are still expected to prove that man is the kind of being we have affirmed him to be. We look to them to save our religion from the aggression of ideas essentially incompatible with our faith. Our very confidence in the psychology of religion to maintain our cause is itself a sign of that uncertainty which always prompts the apologetic venture. In this spirit we say, or train men to say for us, " 'Yes,' the universe is a very mysterious affair, 'but' man's religious experience stands in its own right." And here we catch ourselves falling back upon the formula of which we would be rid. We are sprung from the loins of the great liberals. Shall we go on to say that our traditional liberalism is the final religious word, and must be kept inviolate? Are we apologists, after all?

CHAPTER SIX

Whither Liberalism?

———————————————— ‹‹›› ————————————————

If our account of the development of religious ideas
in America has been in any way faithful to the facts,
it is clear that Christianity had nothing more to expect from Puritanism after the middle of the eighteenth century. We have by that time a highly elaborated theology and little or no living religion, since a
God who is everything and man who is nothing do
not constitute a religion. Matters generally follow
this course, and what is at first a religious conviction
with power to fire men's souls becomes with the passage of time a platitude of theology which no longer
has any influence on their lives.

The Great Awakening of the eighteenth century
was not the noisy rattling of the dry bones of Puritanism—even though attended by much moral earn-
estness—which commonly bears that name; the true
awakening was the fresh confidence in man which
was stirring in the minds of men like Mayhew and
Johnson. This liberal revival meant, as we have
already indicated, a revolutionary account of human

nature, rendered more or less inevitable because thought had come to the end of its tether in elaborating the doctrine of the divine sovereignty. It may be an overstatement to say that in the name of religion the first liberals had to turn their backs on God; it is wholly true to say that for the sake of religion they had to ignore the kind of God in whom tradition required them to believe, and to occupy their minds with other matters, in this instance their own affairs.

We do not imply for a moment that this first liberalism was either atheistic or agnostic, merely that it occupied itself quite properly with getting man back onto the stage. Liberals from that day to this have generally professed belief in God; at the same time God has not been the real center of their interest and what they thought about him has been conditioned by other and prior ideas. A liberal Christian has been a man who thought well of both himself and his fellow men. Given the long prior prohibition of this right, we cannot question the propriety of his thoughts. For man had more than a right, he had a duty to think better of himself than Puritanism had let him think.

We have had by this time, however, two hundred years of liberal thinking about ourselves, with the result that we stand at the opposite pole of the religious paradox from that of our Puritan forefathers.

If religion was in danger of dying two centuries ago because it had been turned into a divine monopoly, religion may be in equal danger of dying today for the contrary reason, that we have made it too much our own affair.

It is hard for us to realize how effectually our long training in liberalism has alienated us from the world order around us. We might say in a sentence that the normal modern man would much rather live in the city than in the country; he understands the stirring and familiar affairs of men much better than the remote "goings-on" of nature, to use Wordsworth's phrase. Matthew Arnold spoke as the perfect liberal when he said that only restless fools aspire to be in harmony with nature, since "nature and man can never be fast friends." Subsequent liberal thinking has widened this felt schism between man and his world until many liberals have now concluded that there is no environment with which we can be fast friends. Man is aware of the world around him; within meager manageable limits he uses it for his own purposes, yet he finds it hard to have any meditative communion with it. An increasing number of modern men feel racially very much alone in the universe. There is about the latest forms of the religious consciousness that same half-anxious intentness and heightened self-consciousness which we know when we are lost in some wild and dreary waste of nature. Humanity, so construing its spiritual lot, is like a man come to a sudden standstill in the middle of a trackless forest. A vivid awareness of ourselves drums in our minds like a relentless tattoo, and all that is around us seems infinitely alien and remote. Having chosen, for better or for worse, to make the principle of personality the first article in our liberal creed, we find little welcome in what Huxley calls "the passionless impersonality of the unknown and the unknowable."

Hence the familiar dilemma of the modern liberal Christian who does not know what to believe about God. Given the intensely human concerns to which he has devoted himself for two hundred years, this is not surprising. Men today do not know what to think about God, for the simple reason that they do not habitually think about God at all. God has passed out of the faith precisely because he has passed out of the mind. Now the idea of God, whatever its content may be, is plainly one of such scope that an occasional five minutes of perplexed wonder does not suffice to give it life in the mind. Those things are real to us which occupy our thought constantly. The indictment of the idolater in the prophecy of Isaiah and again in the parallel passage in the Wisdom of Solomon is not so much a criticism of his worship of the idol itself as of the meager place which his god had in his life. The idolater whittled a god out of the odds and ends of his sticks in the odds and ends of his time. He took a piece of wood and first made the vessels that he needed for daily use; he then built a fire with the better part of the shavings and baked his bread; the god got what was left—"the very refuse among those which served no use . . . when he had nothing else to do." The resultant idea of God was not very real.

Liberalism has been busy for a century or more carving out serviceable utensils for human uses. Many of these utensils are still in the rough and much work remains to be done. Men have been convinced that they hear the voice of God most clearly in the voice of humanity, and therefore the race has been content to conduct in the name of religion its own dramatic monologue. The supposition that there can be a waiting and prophetic half of religion in the desert "where no man is; the wilderness where there is no man," passes our liberal imagining.

Now the logical conclusion of liberalism is not latitude or tolerance in creedal matters; it is humanism. If a group of persons choose to associate themselves together religiously on the basis of the private right of each to believe what he likes, there is no external authority to forbid such a society calling itself a liberal church. That is indeed the present vernacular meaning of the term and it is so employed by all those churches which stress the rights of private conscience in matters of faith and conduct. This is, however, a use of the term which the more consistent non-theological liberals of the last century would not have recognized. Liberalism is not so much a lack of beliefs or idiosyncrasy in believing, as a particular kind of belief. The authentic liberal has a creed and a very noble creed at that; its first article is, "I believe in man." We shall do the history of modern thought much service if we sharpen our theological definition of liberalism and bring it into line with the great cultural tradition which bears that name. For this reason we say that the humanist is, in the strict meaning of the term, the truest religious liberal of the present day. Having said that, we do not ask whether humanism is to be the religion of the future, but rather, whether liberalism still retains its original religious vigor. This is the major cultural issue, of which the "humanist controversy" is a minor ecclesiastical aspect.

As I see these matters the humanist is, on his own premises, well within his rights in saying that hereafter man "may have to rely on himself in religion," since by its own profession "humanism is faith in the supreme value and perfectibility of human personality." This attribution of "supreme value" to man is an unequivocal statement and leaves no room for any higher value in the universe, hence words such as these are the perfect antithesis of all that was affirmed by the prior Puritan creed. The humanist is, however, wrong in saying that humanism "is not simply another denomination . . . it is a new type of religion altogether. It is a new way of looking at religion." This assumption of novelty, if it implies that twentieth-century humanism is a genuine innovation, betrays grave ignorance of much past thought, particularly during the nineteenth century. One would suppose that Comte, Feuerbach, and Harrison had never lived and spoken about these matters at all. Since the jaded American public loves to feed upon novelties the clerical humanist may be well advised to play up the apparent novelty of his dogmas and profit by the patronage which novelty invites, but he is either willfully or ignorantly confusing the issues when he says his religion is new. For myself I can find no important statement in contemporary religious humanism that has not been anticipated and cannot be matched by similar and, on the whole, more adequate statements from the great liberals of the nineteenth century.

Therefore the humanists in our churches are not, as I see them, prophets pointing to the dawn; they are reflective persons sitting down in the late afternoon of a long day, trying to tie up the loose ends of liberal thought and to bring its affairs to something like a decent conclusion. Humanism seems to me to be, in the history of Christian thought, much the same sort of phenomenon as later Calvinism was, differing in this one important respect, that it is an exactly antithetical statement of the truth of religion. It is a grave historical error to regard the religious humanism of the moment as a manifestation of that "freshness of the early world" which we always find when religion is being born or reborn. The humanist is not a trail-blazer; he is a reflective theologian, a late systematic thinker who is drawing from the whole history of liberalism its final logical conclusions. There was a day when liberalism was a religion, but liberalism has now passed out of its spontaneous stage into its reflective stage. When this change came it is hard to say; Morley says that it came politically in England at the end of the nineteenth century with the Boer War. In America we gave lip service a few years later to the theory that we were still trying "to make the world safe for democracy," but vast numbers of persons said the words with the tongue in the cheek, and there was abroad a profound skepticism as to the power of this platitude to work the desired result. A man is no longer ostracized from the company of thoughtful persons if his ears are deaf to the worn-out rhetoric of republicanism. For this reason we say that culturally and in the world of affairs liberalism is ceasing to be a religion and, in so far as it survives at all, survives in its reflective theological state.

Meanwhile within the ranks of liberalism heresy is already making its appearance. The theological rebels of the eighteenth century, doubting the dogma of man's miserable nature and more miserable destiny, affirmed their faith in his right to be happy. The heresy in our day will be therefore a doubt as to man's right to happiness. That phrase is so much a part of the current orthodoxy of liberalism that it does not occur to most of us to regard it as open to question, yet once it has been challenged it is, like all theological axioms, difficult to prove.

This heresy is already lifting its head in more than one quarter. Orthodox Christians in England have long known that L. P. Jacks would undoubtedly "perish everlastingly," in accordance with the damnatory conclusion to the Athanasian Creed. But now conventional liberals find that he does not hold the pure faith of their persuasion, either. I quote from his most recent utterance on these matters,

I regard the quest for happiness as the most unfortunate enterprise on which the human race has ever embarked. Most of the miseries of mankind are attributable to it. Three parts of the suffering which men have inflicted on one another, the long record of man's inhumanity to man, wars, persecutions, cruelties and the rest of it, have their source in some fool's "secret of happiness."

Whenever the quest for happiness becomes dominant in an age or civilization we find that the music and colour die out of life, the arts languish, wisdom perishes, joy departs, class is set against class, and men take to quarrelling with one another like fiends.

They quarrel for a very simple reason. Starting out with the notion that all men have the "right" to happiness (the kind of nonsense talked by Rousseau and in the preamble to the American Declaration of Independence) and finding as they invariably do, that the sort of happiness they demand is not to be had, they naturally conclude that some other fellow has deprived them of it and begin hunting for the villain who has done it, pitching on all kinds of innocent persons, whom they harry and villify and torture and tax, utterly unconscious of the fact that they have only themselves to thank for being such fools as to think they had the right to be "happy."

Nobody has any such right or would be any better off if he had. . . . No human being is fitted for such an existence, either by the constitution of his body or the constitution of his mind. . . . Any God, or Universe, which offered them that as the end-all and goal of their existence, would be a God not worthy of worship, and a universe not worth living in. It would be a universe without meaning, without value, without beauty, the silliest and most contemptible universe the mind can conceive; a fool's paradise, if you like, but a hell for everybody except the fools, and not much of a paradise even for them. . . . So then, if anybody asks me, "What is your secret of happiness?" my answer is, "I have none."*

*L. P. Jacks, quoted from a recent article in "The Daily Mail."

In these vigorous words there is not a shred of liberalism left. Judged by the uninterrupted liberal tradition of the past two centuries, Dr. Jacks is here discovered to be, as he clearly intends to be, a prophet of illiberalism. He represents that type of mind in the modern world which has passed clean through the intellectual and moral discipline of liberalism, has exhausted its possibilities, and has turned in another direction to look for the revival of religion. As he has said more than once, in the name of religion he will have nothing to do with that latest dogmatic theology known as humanism, since he does not believe that living religion at the present time can be sought or found there.

The hope of a religious revival in the near future lies, then, neither with the elder orthodoxy, nor with the traditional liberal; it lies with that person whom we must describe as the illiberal liberal. Orthodoxy and all that we mean by Fundamentalism, which still abides by the remnants of the Puritan system, must sooner or later pass through its own liberal stage; it must experience in its own mind and members that gracious humanizing of thought and interest which made the ample nineteenth century what it was. We are concerned here, however, with the person who belongs to that cultural and religious tradition which we identify as liberalism. These persons now seem nearly to have exhausted the first religious energy of their distinctive idea. There still remains a good deal to be done by way of vindicating the worth and dignity of man latent in oppressed peoples, submerged classes, backward races, the mentally incompetent, the industrially unfit, and the morally perverse. To call liberalism off its day's work when that work is only begun may seem treason to the simple gospel, a turning back when the hand has been put to the plough. Yet everyone whose interests bring him constantly into touch with these direct endeavors to improve the race realizes that what we call "social service"—the faith of liberalism translated into works—is ceasing to be a religious vocation and is becoming an organized secular profession. The distinctive religious quality in the characters of the great liberators and reformers of the nineteenth century is wanting in the men who are now our professional philanthropists. Modern social service is still conscientiously done, yet it is too often uninspired and uninspiring: it is liberalism "carrying on." The idealistic, missionary, sacrificial spirit which sustained it a generation or so ago has for some reason passed away. This does not mean that the work is not being done and on the whole well and patiently done, but that the reasons for doing it and the manner of doing it are no longer recognized as being distinctively religious. These tasks have become part of the day's work of the world. The historians, sociologists, economists, and psychologists who isolate the problems and then propose their solution are not, in so far as they associate themselves with religion, our prophets; they are our modern theologians, and the clearest headed of them would be the first to acknowledge this. They are dealing with the science of liberal religion as that religion has been handed over to them by the century and a half before our own.

All of us who have to do with younger people know that this old social-service motive has for the moment lost its appeal to youth. In our critical and more ungenerous moments we are inclined to think that modern youth is selfish, and in our haste we pillory it for its want of social conscience and vision. Yet, if we know our next generation well, we come slowly to realize that this is so precisely because liberalism is a theology not a religion, and that every oncoming generation is right to discriminate between bread and a stone. What may have been once a religion to us has become a theology to them, and they must have a living religion; not merely some reflective science of religion, even though it be the correct sociological or psychological model of the current year.

For many years now I have listened to class after class delivering sermons in a theological school. No themes are prescribed and students are encouraged to preach upon subjects that interest them. When I was in the seminary we had a single subject around which or at which we preached, "Is the ethic of Jesus practicable?" This was the one absorbing topic indicated and required by a late liberalism, and its prominence in our minds classified us as the children of liberalism. The school with which I am now connected is not usually identified as being theologically backward and is indeed supposed to be in the forefront of the modern movement. But it has been many years now since I have heard a single sermon preached by a student, which deals with that question which was uppermost in our minds at the beginning of the century. I have found myself asking, Do these men who are going out into the churches not care about those matters which once seemed so vital to us? Are they going to pass by the victims on the Jericho road of history, as modern priests and Levites? I know them too well to indict them wholesale; their candor and integrity forbid the instinctive ungenerous judgment. Well, what do they preach about, then? They have been trying to find out whether there is a God, and if so what He is like. Few or none of them have reverted to conventional orthodoxy, some of them are agnostic, some of them are still airing the ancient grudge against orthodoxy, others of them are facing a great mystery with reverent hope and trust, but they are all alike concerned with the idea of God.

As I reflect on the contrast between the ideas which were abroad in the seminary in the days when I was a divinity student and those which are abroad now among the younger men with whom I work, I am driven to the conclusion that it is I who had not found the religious range, not they. By contrast they seem to me to be seeking, and in some measure finding, the truth of religion, to better purpose than the men of my student time. I realize in retrospect that I put through my divinity school training, passed on into the active ministry, and spent some years in that ministry in utter want of any real concern for the idea of God. I can mark the day, one of the outstanding days in my lifelong process of being converted to religion, when all that is meant by this idea ceased to be a hereditary fiction or a remote hypothesis and became a reality. I had been for some time assistant minister to an old man in a mill-city parish. Once each year he preached a stated sermon on the discoveries in astronomy during the previous twelve months. The sermon was long, and often technical

beyond our terrestrial wit and patience. On a certain
Monday morning following this sermon I went into
his study, filled with the spirit of propagandist liberalism, and entered my protest in the form of a question. I said with some conviction, "Here is this city
where everybody is busy making and selling cotton
cloth, I can't see the use to these people of your
yearly sermon on astronomy." He smiled and said
with a fine freedom, "My dear boy, of course it is
no use at all, but it greatly enlarges my idea of God."
That stray remark lighted up a whole area of which
I had been until that time utterly unaware. I walked
out of his study into a world which has never been
since then the same. No one in the seminary had ever
said any such thing to me, illuminated my mind, or
stirred my imagination in that way. But from that
day to this I have known that "greatly enlarged ideas
of God" are supremely necessary to religion and that
in the long run you cannot make good cotton cloth or
sell it honestly in want of such ideas. Concentration
on cotton cloth is not the whole of religion. It seems
a strange thing that one can grow up in a professedly
religious environment, be actively identified with all
kinds of religious activities, choose an avowedly
religious profession, pass through technical prepara-
tion for that profession and be well on in the practice
of the profession without ever being really aware of

God; yet that in substance is what happened to me. It is not that I was indifferent to religion, but that my whole approach to religion was that made by one whose lot fell at a time when liberalism was still the whole of religion. I suspect that my case is not unique. It is for this reason that I listen with interest and gratitude to students preaching in the class-room who seem to me to be correcting my history at the point where it has been deficient and in danger of coming to a point of arrest. I follow their minds with interest and hope.

Now all this is not to say that the time will not again come, for it certainly will come, when some new-born Jonathan Mayhew will have to defend man against an even more imperious "astronomical intimidation" than is now meted out to us. Plainly we shall see at some future day a racial rebellion and successful revolution which once more disallows the monopolistic right of the universe to ride over us rough shod. On another day another Pascal will have to vindicate the "reed that thinks." All this will have to be said over again, in other ways, centuries hence. At the moment, however, there is no religious need to go on repeating this particular dogma, and those who are now saying these things are systematic thinkers, as Edwards, Bellamy, Hopkins, and Dwight were at an earlier time. Faith in the dignity and worth of the human individual, which was once a heresy that carried with it the promise of a revival of religion, is now a theological platitude; and when a truth long reiterated degenerates into a platitude and loses its power of truth, there is no gain to be had in saying it more vociferously or in fuller elaboration; it is time to say something else. That something else which we need to learn how to say is "God." At the risk of flogging our argument to death must we not say that the hope of the religion of tomorrow is in the keeping, neither of the orthodox believer nor of the traditional liberal, but of that man whom for the want of any more accurate designation we must describe as the "illiberal liberal." By this term I mean to suggest the type of person who in his heredity and experience has passed clean through the discipline of the liberalism of the last two centuries, has seen it finally formulated in the dogmatic theology of humanism, and who has no mind to be put off with a dogmatic theology instead of a living religion.

This illiberal liberal is a person with deeply humane sympathies and humanitarian hopes, who despairs of ever fully expressing those sympathies or realizing those hopes unless this be also the cosmic intention. He is, in the terms of our present American life, the man who is learning in political miniature what he expects may be the cosmic truth, that there is no such thing as "splendid isolation." The modern American in the person of his forbears, if not in his own experience, turned his back on the despotisms and absolute monarchies of the Old World. He vindicated the place of a free people in a new land, yet he has not succeeded in isolating himself. Most of the absolute monarchs of the Old World are gone; the nations with their peoples remain, and the sober wisdom of the White House has even now shown us the truth of ourselves; we are irrevocably involved in world affairs, our lot is one with the nations of the whole world. We must go back to the dame school of world history.

Something of the same sort has happened to the religious liberal. His theological revolution was successful and he threw off the absolute divine sovereignty, as he supposed forever. Yet his dream of splendid racial independence has not come true and he finds that, though the old dogmas are gone, a vast residual reality remains from which he cannot isolate himself and with which he is involved. As the wisest American is today the man who knows that we cannot live apart from the elder continents, and as the true political wisdom for the future is in the keeping of this un-American American who is not content to go on rehearsing the frayed-out platitudes of a self-sufficient and isolated democracy, so the true religious wisdom of the hour is in the keeping of the illiberal liberal who knows that in the name of religion and for the sake of religion he must turn and face the universe, because he has traffic with it whether he like or not. The fundamentalist in our religion is like some old surviving royalist in our democracy; what he says harks back to a day that is gone beyond recall and he has little to contribute to the future. On the other hand, as Fourth of July oratory of the conventional type has become hollow and irrelevant, so dogged and faithful insistence upon "the dignity and worth of the individual" with his "right to happiness" is not enough for today. If this dignity and worth and happiness are or are to become ultimate realities, they cannot be vindicated in the 100-per-cent racial patriotism of those who still celebrate their splendid human isolation. Either we are involved in and with the universe or religion is the ultimate delusion.

I do not imply that it will be easy to begin saying "God" clearly and unequivocally. The word, as representing an austere reality constantly present in the mind, is not a familiar one. It took our liberal forefathers a century to learn to say "man" plainly and fully. They had to fumble with the word at first and found its meanings and promises slowly. It may well take our time quite as long to learn again how to say "God." A century ago Cardinal Newman, still standing in the elder tradition, said, "Nothing is easier than to say 'God' and mean nothing by it." Our age refuses to say "God" in that way, and its long silence is a pledge of its determination not to say it thus. If men hesitate today to take that word upon their lips too easily, this reticence is the pledge of a new sincerity; when we speak the word again it shall be more than an ancient platitude. It may well be that a waiting agnosticism, an agnosticism which is expectant rather than despairing, is necessary before the word gains its newer and truer meanings in our time. The name of the covenant God of Israel was never spoken in later Judaism; the Jews made use of a periphrasis. True, this reticence sprang from a technical fear of idolatry and profanation of the divine reality, yet in those golden silences of the scroll of the law and the prophets there was a profound religious wisdom. What matters is not that we should say "God" too soon or too easily, what matters is that we should know that this is the one word above all others which any religion must utter and that we should be trying to learn how to say it.

CHAPTER SEVEN

The Greatness and Littleness of Man

————————————‹‹››————————————

In an earlier chapter we said something about the religious maturity of the gospels. That maturity we identified as a matter of just proportion between the greatness of God and the greatness of man. Such works are very rare, since most religious books are partisan briefs for either God's sovereignty or man's rights.

There is, however, one book in our tradition which gives us this same impression of spiritual maturity, the *Thoughts* of Blaise Pascal. Pascal's thoughts were far more sophisticated than those of Jesus, and in their form they are much nearer to this century than to the first century. Though he lived and wrote in the seventeenth century, Pascal foresaw with an uncanny clarity those contradictions by which the mind of later times was to be torn, therefore the *Thoughts* is a book at once religiously mature and modern.

These meditations play around a single idea, the greatness and the littleness of man. When he consults himself, says Pascal, man knows that he is great;

when he contemplates the universe around him he knows that he is little, and his ultimate greatness consists in this knowledge of his littleness.

It is hard at this distance to discover in his life the sources of this paradox which is the core of Pascal's religion. He had been as a young man a mathematician and physicist of the first rank; his work in these fields was both original and important. He had, therefore, even in that seventeenth century, something of the dispassionate and objective mind of the modern scientist. He was, on the other hand, an ardent disciple of Montaigne and owed to that master his strong strain of humanistic interest, an affection for and a confidence in human nature. On his conversion he cast his lot with the Jansenists of Port Royal and therefore identified himself for the moment with the more objective account of religion. But he was never a blind partisan, wholly of the Port Royal persuasion; he was "in and out" of Jansenism. During the years that followed his conversion, as in the days before his conversion, two men struggled within him for the mastery—the pure scientist and the humanist. Neither of these men ever won a decisive victory; one of them had only to gain a temporary advantage for the other to reassert himself with fresh vigor. It is this constant tension between two minds, one scientifically disinterested and the other humanely interested, which gives to Pascal's character and works their peculiar religious maturity. If Pascal never resolved the contradiction, at least he understood of what elemental stuff the religious consciousness is compounded. We can get, at this late date, little technical theological help from Pascal's *Thoughts*; we can still draw from it profound religious insights.

Pascal seems to be, therefore, the type of man whom, for the want of any more accurate term, we must classify as an illiberal liberal. I mean by this term that he conceded at first and to the full the liberal doctrine of the greatness of man. This greatness he conceived to be an immediate fact, something that is given in man as man. This genial side of his character, which drew from Montaigne a certain love of the world and joy in human society, a strong confidence in man's ability to manage skillfully his own affairs, an almost mystical devotion to the miracle of self-consciousness—all this marks Pascal as a liberal and a humanist. We might say that he anticipated and even lived through the age of liberalism in his own experience, having, as some men seem to have, a strange power to compress long periods of history within the short limits of a single life.

There was, however, another and entirely different side to Pascal which is reflected in his meditations on the littleness of man. I know of no other writer who can give one as instantly and as completely, an intimation of the vast reaches of time and space that surround us. The idea of infinity was always with him, and since he was a mathematician this idea had content; it was not mere vacuity or indeterminateness. Infinity was with him a positive rather than a negative fact. He looks out always with wonder and often with a nameless dread at what a later writer calls this *mysterium tremendum*. This is, however, a reasonable and holy fear always under control, not the panic of animal fright; whatever the universe might do to him, Pascal knew that he could always be his own man. Yet it was in the presence of the infinities that he learned the sober lesson of his littleness. This side of Pascal is patently illiberal, since it is entirely wanting in any humanistic self-confidence or self-congratulation. Pascal does not so much deny his humanism as set it in its final relation to the universe, and it seems to be his mature judgment that man's true greatness is to be found not in a forthright humanism, but in his ability to go far afield from that humanism. Pascal had two conversions to religion; the first was apparently imperfect, the second complete. We might say that he was converted to the religion of humanism as he pondered himself and other men, and then reconverted to it more accurately in the presence of those infinities which his mind could neither penetrate nor escape. He was, like Job, the sort of man whom the universe commands to stand and reckon with it, and, again like Job, a man who felt that he had his own measure much more truly after that reckoning than before.

It is for these reasons that I have classified him as an illiberal liberal, a humanist, it is true, yet not merely a humanist; a humanist plus. . . . And that "plus" which was necessary to his mature and perfected humanism was supplied by the outer order of things and what that order had to say of itself; his final faith was not affirmed by pitching his first faith a note higher and trying to drown out the music of the spheres with the shrillness of his own voice.

Now I venture to think that "the religion of the future," whatever we may mean or whatever may be meant by that phrase in which we vest so much hope, will be an illiberal liberalism of this sort. We can no more deny or ignore the religious history of the last two hundred years than Pascal could forget what he had learned from Montaigne. It is stuff of our very stuff and life of our life, which cannot be eradicated. This latest phase of humanitarian emphasis in religion which we call modern liberalism is one through which all the historic faiths must pass in due time.

On the other hand, liberalism, particularly in its

theological elaboration as humanism, can no more remain the whole of religion in our time than Puritanism could have remained the whole of religion two hundred years ago. The universe will reassert itself, indeed has been reasserting itself in our minds in these last years. It refuses to be banished from our thought, it challenges our power to know it, and stirs our wonder as we ponder it. The man who realizes this and turns now to face that universe, which in his humanistic preoccupations he has ignored so long, is our illiberal liberal. He is the man who is already prophesying the religion of tomorrow, and all that is permanently valid in the religion of liberalism will finally be conserved by him as he discovers our true greatness in the measure of our racial littleness.

Church historians in their researches into the past have learned to look for the first signs of a new revival of religion not among the formal affairs of churchmen and theologians, but more often than otherwise in the cultural interests of the lay world around. It is among men who are "unsubsidised"— to use Mark Rutherford's word once more—that we usually detect the first spontaneous movements of the free spirit. Churches are necessary to conserve and to consolidate religious experiences that men have already had; we cannot uniformly find out what is going to happen by consulting churches. Now what strikes one about the present moment is the appearance in many quarters of the temper which I have called illiberal liberalism; on the whole, this temper is the most arresting fact in the cultural scene. There are three or four manifestations of this illiberality which are worth noticing; they are significant because they mark what is for the moment the most characteristic and vital thing in our life, a new outward-mindedness. These concerns have no theological form as yet; indeed, they make no direct claim to be religious in substance, yet they plainly reveal a tendency of the unforsworn human spirit to move away from the world within toward the world without. Three such facts deserve mention: a more objective art, a genuine and widespread interest in what Jeans calls "the universe around us," a new note of disinterestedness in morality. I do not claim for a moment that any or all of these as they stand are sufficient to give us religion, but I am persuaded that they intimate at this particular moment the direction in which we are to seek religion and the sources from which we may expect it. By contrast I think that further strained elaboration of liberalism in the form of humanism is doomed to be a second-hand affair, a formal theological afterthought. Whatever fresh wind of the spirit blows in our faces comes from this other quarter.

There is first of all the present drift of the arts. Nothing is plainer here than the spent quality of romanticism. It survives today mainly in its spurious and degenerate forms of sentimentalism, and even its authentic classics of yesterday, when seen or read or heard again, do not fit the tempers of this age. For the moment we have got beyond that. The truth is that this vein was well worked through the last century; all man's normal emotions received during that time fair and full statement. In order to keep up our traditional concern for human nature we have had to turn aside to its abnormalities, and even our curiosity about these begins to flag, since the permutations and combinations of the perversions are very limited. In so far as we are forced to admit that our present normal interest in human nature is an interest in its abnormalities we suspect this state of affairs, for this is not what liberalism intended or what liberalism meant; confidence in the dignity and worth of man cannot be equated as a prurient curiosity about his less dignified and more unlovely aspects. This is romanticism gone stale, diseased, dying.

I have been much struck, for example, by the way in which ultra-modern young people like to listen to Haydn and Bach and Mozart. They are meanwhile frankly bored by Wagner or Schumann, and skeptical of Brahms; even Beethoven is a border-line case.

These are the selfsame young people whose reading is uncensored and unafraid, whose talk is painfully frank, and whose ethics are said to be wholly unconventional. It is not easy to fit these two parts of the picture together. Why should they prefer the formal measures of Mozart to the soul-revealing, heart-breaking passion of some Wagner hero or heroine? I suspect that it is because these same young people have their own human measure more accurately than the romanticists had that measure. They have become realists about themselves, and once they have become realistic the romantic game is up. They belong to an age for which self-expression has done both its best and its worst; like another rather disillusioned humanist, they are "weary of themselves and sick of asking what they are and what they ought to be."

For this reason they turn to some cool objective medium to reassure and to find themselves. They know all about their own emotions; they are impatient of the hereditary dogma of liberalism which bids them "make something of themselves"—tell them this, they blandly ask you, "Why?" and since that statement is an axiom it is not easy to explain or prove. In their persons a certain erosion of thorough-going skepticism is at work on the whole liberal-romantic orthodoxy of the past hundred years or more. Their new thoughts are as unintelligible to us as the thoughts that Jonathan Mayhew had two hundred years ago were unintelligible to his Puritan contemporaries. He simply looked at the whole Puritan theology and asked, "Why?" This was a heretical question from a courageous young man, and since no one could answer it, liberalism became inevitable. So, at the other pole of the paradox these young people of our own time, who are the surest sign of the time, seem to be turning in art to a much more objective account of life than has been current in the near past.

There are two possible theories of æsthetics. One is that proposed by the critics of a century or more ago, who founded it upon the association of ideas. They said that the objects which we think beautiful have no beauty in themselves, but remind us of past pleasures of our own, and by stirring again our old emotions become beautiful to us. This is the doctrine of emotion recollected in tranquillity which underlies the romantic, subjective account of beauty. Thus, I think the "Daffodils" a beautiful poem not because it is in itself a lovely word structure, but because it reminds me of the flowers which used to grow beside a lake near my boyhood home and so reawakens the emotions of my childhood. Whatever rouses past emotion in me by this process of associated ideas I think beautiful and from it I draw pleasure. On this theory the sense of beauty is merely a tranquil recollection of my own past feelings, a highly subjective transaction.

The other theory of beauty, older and also newer, holds that we get æsthetic pleasure from the contemplation of parts fitly arranged in a symmetrical and unified whole. Thus, I find the temple at Segesta beautiful not because it reminds me of the New England meeting-house to which I went as a boy and thus recovers for me the lost feelings of childhood's joys; I find it beautiful for what it is in itself, a perfectly proportioned work in stone. The perception of its perfect symmetry gives me an intellectual pleasure which is not dependent upon any personal association for its strength. So the pleasure which I get from a Bach fugue does not derive from dead emotions of mine which it has again called into life. It does not remind me of cradle songs or of college songs, or of a wedding march, or of a funeral dirge, or of battle hymns; none of my past feelings of joy or sorrow are awakened by that fugue. In fact, I find it very hard to connect Bach with my own feelings in any way, yet he stirs an immediate emotion of pleasure, because I am arrested by the total orderliness of the vagrant voices of his fugues. He resolves in my hearing the riddle of the parts and the whole, and because he does so I say that his music is beautiful. This is probably what is meant by that term "significant form" which modern art critics use to suggest the main concern of modern art; the thing-in-itself is interesting, lovely, and of independent worth. The beautiful object does not have to have "my vote to be so if it can"—in Browning's words; it is so in its own right. Thus, we put down this new objectivity in art as one of the more suggestive facts in modern life, not without its prophetic meaning for religion.

There is next the "mysterious universe" which is "around us." George Tyrrell once wrote to a friend, "I am afraid that you do not study the stars enough." That has been the chronic weakness of liberalism and romanticism, as it remains the grave deficiency of humanism. Meanwhile the number of persons who have suddenly become interested in the stars is growing by leaps and bounds. My old father-in-God in that mill-city parish would find today, were he still alive and at work, a much readier hearing for his annual sermon on astronomy than he found twenty-five years ago. Why is it that magazines now make a constant place in their pages for reliable popular articles on astronomy? Why is it that Jeans and Eddington become best sellers overnight? This is a question which those who are concerned with religion will do well to ponder. I suggest that it is because humanitarianism and humanism are not enough to satisfy all the capacities of the human mind, and that these popular accounts of vast and mysterious matters minister to an actual spiritual need in our souls. I cannot believe that all this is sheer idle curiosity, for idle curiosity would not incite tired business and professional men to wrestle with such books when the day's work is over, if they did not meet a deeply felt want. Nor can the psychiatrist persuade me that by reading about the stars we compensate in our own eyes for our littleness and achieve a vicarious magnitude from these immensities, though I recognize the type of mind which employs large talk to conceal its own ignorance. I must think that we have turned to these considerations with a certain hunger, partly mental, but in equal part emotional and moral, precisely because we men are not enough for ourselves.

I have cited Pascal as an illiberal liberal, I would add Wordsworth to the list, for it is this same sense of an unresolved contradiction running through Wordsworth's poetry which gives to it its peculiarly religious quality. Humanism never had finer statement than in the last lines of the sonnet to Toussaint L'Ouverture,

> Thou hast great allies,
> Thy friends are exultations, agonies,
> And love, and man's unconquerable mind.

Wordsworth never doubted or denied that the divine which is deeply interfused in things dwells "in the mind of man"; that was indeed the original article of his creed as it remained its first article, which marks him for all time one of the great liberals of the last century. Yet his liberalism was constantly turning illiberal, for he could not escape the conviction that this something far more deeply interfused dwells also in

> The light of setting suns,
> And the round ocean, and the living air,
> And the blue sky. . . .
> And rolls through all things.

Like Pascal he found man's greatness in man's knowledge of his littleness, and it was his mature faith that

> Our destiny, our being's heart and home
> Is with infinitude, and only there.

Whether our heart's home is with the infinities around us we do not know, humanism prefers to ignore these infinities in behalf of our racial housekeeping. And yet many a truant humanist buys a volume by Jeans or Eddington, just because he cannot get away from the suspicion that his destiny is in some way bound up with the universe. If I were a thorough-going humanist I should see to it that such cosmic themes as these were denied my followers; I should be more careful to suppress them than are the makers of the Roman Index to suppress liberal Protestant books, for they contain the germs of the ultimate heresy.

So, also, I am interested in what Einstein has to say about religion, though I do not profess to understand the subtleties of the theory of relativity. What I can understand is Einstein's simple account of his religious faith. By his own confession he believes in what he calls "cosmic religion." He finds this religion intimated in the Psalms of David and in the Prophets. He overhears it in Saint Francis' *Canticle to Brother Sun.* "The individual feels the vanity of human desires and aims, and the nobility of the marvellous orders which are revealed in nature and in the world of thought." The greatness of man who is thus little lies in his power to lay his mind faithfully alongside the universe that is infinite; this is his only greatness. Einstein says that this highest religious experience is found only among the heretics of all ages; be that as it may, "cosmic religion" must be for the modern humanist what Modernism itself was for the Catholic Church, not merely a heresy, but "the sum of all heresies." Einstein's mind has nothing in common with the religions of liberalism and humanism, being at the crucial point utterly and consistently illiberal. Yet I venture to suggest that he catches our attention and stirs our imagination, as do his fellow workers, Jeans and Eddington and Michelson, precisely because there is more in us than can be satisfied by a purely humanistic religion; some prompting which persuades us that "our being's heart and home is with infinitude." This general and popular interest in vast considerations, which the lay mind follows only stumblingly at the best, is a clear intimation that the patriotic religion of humanity "is not enough" and that we are glad and willing to have the objective universe reassert itself in our minds.

None of these men who are pioneering for us in these infinities say "God" unequivocally; indeed, some of them deny that the word ever can be said with reference to their findings. That seems to me to be beside the mark, for the moment. It may well be that some new period of reverent wonder will be necessary before we reach another time of definition when we can speak the name of God with a fuller confidence in its newer and truer meanings. What matters is that we concede at this moment that it is useless to look for a God within unless also we are also willing to seek Him without. To know that we seek reality there as well as here is half our battle. We must learn not to be afraid of a tentative agnosticism, if necessary, since too neat and sufficient definitions of liberalism as a theology have taught us the peril of all theologies which have lost touch with their occasioning religion. In short, the illiberal liberal may not always understand the new physics or the new astronomy of our day, but he trusts the direction in which such a mind faces, and looks in that direction with eager hope.

Then there is that matter of ethical dispassionateness. Mr. Lippmann in his much-discussed book, *A Preface to Morals*, tells us that disinterestedness, dispassionateness, are to be the heart of the high religion of the future. He classifies himself as a humanist, though I question the classification. He chooses the term because he cannot believe in the kind of arbitrary autocrat whom orthodox Jews and orthodox Christians have called God. He does not believe there is any such being. Since he is patently a religiously minded man he wishes a religion of some sort, and for the want of any better term he accepts the humanist label.

But his insistence upon the ethical importance of disinterestedness is itself a question mark set upon the propriety of his religious self-designation. It is true that men may achieve an increasingly disinterested service of one another, but they cannot make a spiritual living by taking in each other's wash of disinterestedness. There must be some positive racial interest into which all this disinterestedness can be metamorphosed. I may be a necessary cog in the social machine and may draw much moral strength from that knowledge, but once let me suspect that the whole machine is merely idling, getting nowhere, achieving nothing, and my moral energy flags at once. There is no humanitarian answer to the skeptical question, "Why should I perpetuate the race?" Religion always supplies a better reason than that— it says that we are a part of some cosmic concern, and even though we do not understand it clearly we are persuaded that harmony with the will of God, whatever that may mean, is reason enough for living a disinterested life.

Thus the disinterestedness of an Einstein is nearer to what religion ought to be than the disinterestedness of a philanthropist who manages to be reasonably selfless, yet suspects all the time that his selflessness will come to nothing in the end. We employ the ethical principle of disinterestedness most fitly not when we confine it to one another, since a perpetual "After you, my dear sir," defeats itself, but when we address it, as pure science addresses it, to the objective universe. So construed, the Stoic affirmation, "Whatsoever is good for thee, O World, is good for me," is a more religious affirmation than an advertisement to the effect that we are always ready to take in each other's humanitarian washing.

One classifies Mr. Lippmann, then, with the physicists and astronomers rather than with the humanists, since plainly the deeper sympathies of his mind are with selflessness rather than self-interest. He has stated as a religious principle a truth which they are stating in the terms of pure science, his is the kind of conduct required by their knowledge. I am, therefore, unable to share in the pious regrets meted out to the *Preface to Morals*, since it seems to me a book much needed as a correction of a too interested morality, a significant religious adventure in illiberal liberalism. The moral core of the book is essentially mystical, though the doctrinal theology falls short of that which most churches require. What really matters in the book is its fresh orientation, its candid break with the ethics of Manchester liberalism. It may have been true for the past hundred years that what Manchester says today the rest of the liberal world will say tomorrow. But Manchester now having said all that it has to say or can say, we are grateful to Mr. Lippmann for saying something else which holds a real promise of ethical reinvigoration.

These three items in the modern scene, chosen quite at random and yet having much in common, I offer as worth consideration in connection with religion. They all betray a new concern for a more objective account of faith and practice. They may not be articulately religious as yet, nevertheless they prophesy religion to come.

Prudential considerations suggest that the liberal would be well advised to cultivate just now some such corrective illiberality; for the liberal period of human history through which we have passed has ended in a time of perplexity and near-chaos. It seems a strange thing that the modern liberal world which has thought so well of itself should have done so badly by itself. There can have been few past times when happiness was as inaccessible to most human beings as it is today and must remain for an indefinite future. The world is unsettled and unhappy to a degree that sobers us. The dogma of liberalism has not worked, and we ask whether this is because the right to happiness has been overstated. Be these matters as they may, liberalism, widespread throughout the Western World, was not able to prevent the war. Whether it was in any way responsible for occasioning the war only some historian of a much later time can say.

There is at this point a religious lesson to be

learned from the life of Wordsworth. His greatest poetry was written just as the eighteenth century passed over into the nineteenth. It was, in the conventional sense of the term, nature poetry, but it was a very mature and twice-born kind of nature poetry, which presupposed an intense interior history.

Wordsworth had had, up to the time he began his best work, a varied life. His parents had died when he was a child. His orphaned boyhood had been passed in a school in the Lake District. He spent three or four desultory years at Cambridge, which academically came to little or nothing. He idled in London and tramped through France. He was finally caught in the tide of French revolutionary interest and carried away by its humanitarian and republican doctrines. Natural rights and liberal hopes ran like an ichor in his system. He fell in love with a certain Annette Vallon and became the father of an illegitimate child. He returned to England only to see his nation involved in a war against France which denied all that he believed. He wandered a semi-fugitive in the deep country; he joined the Jacobins in secret meetings; he seems even to have been spied on by the government. Then Dorothy found him, took him back to the Lake District, and there he saluted the dear earth that had begot him.

His life was at that time on the verge of breaking

up into shattered fragments. It had been discontinuous and without any "central peace" or unity; it was
meaningless and essentially irreligious because it
lacked simplicity—singleness. His problem was how
to unify his life, the problem to which all religion
addresses itself. There was no obvious principle of
unity within; only discontinuity, disharmony, chaos.

By some miracle Dorothy "gave him eyes"; she
made him look at the world around him, and as he
gazed he became aware of the constancy and orderliness of that world. There were the same hills and
tarns he had loved years before. This identity of
nature reassured him as to the still inviolate integrity
of his own soul—he was the same man, and despite
his vicissitudes he was one man. Thus he looks at
one of the lovely and constant facts in nature and
says,

> So was it when my life began;
> So is it now I am a man;
> So be it when I shall grow old;
>   Or let me die!
>
> I could wish my days to be
> Bound each to each by natural piety.

This natural piety was a "central peace," first found
in the universe and then reflected in his own spiritual
history. Wordsworth, therefore, did not gain this

religious reassurance by introspection; he learned it from the outer world of which he became newly aware in maturity and with which he believed himself to be in some vital way identified. That experience is worth pondering as an example of illiberal liberalism.

The trouble with our modern world is just this; it lacks natural piety. There is apparently available, in the terms of racial introspection, no reassurance as to the integrity and peaceable order of human history or human society. Recent history has been discontinuous spiritually, and has led us to the brink of cultural chaos. Every one realizes how uncertain most of the states of modern life are. It is better here than in Europe and Asia, but it is bad everywhere, and our seeming American security is increasingly involved in the general insecurity. Where to get that natural piety which the modern world needs is a riddle that baffles liberalism. Certainly if liberalism ever had the secret of that piety it seems now to have lost it.

This natural piety, in so far as it is being assured to us at all, comes to us from the objective type of mind which we have been reviewing. Classes in "International Relations" will not of themselves solve our problem; we need classes in more objective matters which require a greater dispassionateness. Tyrrell would say this in another way and to even better effect, "I am afraid that you do not study the stars enough." Natural piety is not revealed religion, but we shall get no further revelations of religion without some personal discipline in precisely this natural piety which our time so sorely needs. The secret of that natural piety is in the keeping of our illiberal liberal who sees the way ahead.

CHAPTER EIGHT

The Place of Jesus in His Own Religion

——————————————‹‹››——————————————

The great majority of Christians in all times have held that the doctrine of the divinity of Christ provides the test-case for Christianity, and that those who deny this doctrine remain Christians only on their own recognizance. It is here that the apologetic strain in Christianity asserts itself most vigorously, since orthodox Christians can be relied upon to rally to the defense of this dogma against all comers. Let it be said of a man that he has doubts about the divinity of Christ and most churches will have nothing to do with him. Let him even so much as ask the custodians of the faith what they mean by the phrase, and they will more often than otherwise conceal their uncertainty beneath a guise of pious indignation. This is not, for the moment at least, an area in which clear and honest thought abounds; it is an area dominated by tradition.

We do not question the right of any Christian to defend the doctrine of the divinity of Christ, provided he knows what he is defending. If, however, he does not know what he means by the words, we have reason to doubt the efficacy of his apology. We can only say of him that he is treasuring a sacred formula which has come down to him through the Christian centuries, and which Christianity has regarded as its most peculiar and precious possession. On the other hand, the clearer men have been about the person and work of Jesus, the less inclined they have been to play the apologist in his behalf. Matthew Arnold said a very true thing of Jesus in saying that Jesus is greater than his interpreters. We might go on to add that Jesus is greater than his apologists. This judgment would apply quite as truly to those who have tried to win historical knowledge of the man as to those who hold the high theological doctrine, for there are some figures in history who seem to render the task of the apologist unnecessary, and Jesus is one of those figures. The truth is, however, that apologists are concerned not to defend the historical man against detractors, but to perpetuate a highly elaborated interpretation of his nature or natures.

Our Christology seems to be in a state of arrest, and badly to need a non-apologetic reconsideration. The direct and rational solution of the matter is to say that Jesus was a "mere man," a very good man, but a "mere" man, nevertheless. This solution begs the issue, since it assumes that we know what a mere man is, either actually or potentially. Church fathers like Irenæus and Athanasius were in this respect much bolder than the orthodoxy of our own time; they did not hesitate to say that Christianity aims to make us divine in the same way and to the same degree that Jesus was divine. This was to their thinking the meaning and intention of the Incarnation. There are many Unitarians who could subscribe to the doctrine of the divinity of Christ on these terms and many orthodox Christians who would shrink from what they would regard as the minimizing nature of any such definition of the divinity of Christ.

Carlyle dismissed the controversialists of the fourth century as persons whose heads were filled with chaff and whose hearts were empty and dead. In reply to that judgment we might cite Caird's statement that men do not permanently occupy their minds with unrealities, and that when we find them century after century thinking over some problem, we may be certain that there is a reality hidden and at stake there. So far as Christology is concerned, Caird is plainly nearer right than Carlyle. There has been something at stake here, even though what is at stake may not have been finally stated. What is at stake, among other things, is the nature of mere man. Hence the affirmation that Jesus is mere man is not the end of the matter, but its beginning in another form. This seems to me to be at least one of the errors of refusing to occupy ourselves further with the subject of Christology, for that whole line of speculation is in part an effort to say what may be meant by the term "mere man."

On the other hand, continued and unthinking use of the term "divinity of Christ" implies that we know what we mean by God, and for vast numbers of persons this is not true. The Christological doctrine was formed at a time when the world had, or thought that it had, reasonably accurate accounts of the natures of God and man. Those accounts have proved to be imperfect and inadequate. We do not question the propriety of continuing to discuss the Christological problem; we do affirm the impropriety and ultimately the impossibility of doing so solely with the aid of the material which the early centuries used to build up their doctrine.

Meanwhile historic Christianity thus far has been very largely Christology, and he who would know that history must try to understand this doctrine, or the history will be unintelligible to him; it is the pass key without which he cannot discover its secrets. A Christianity in which Jesus no longer matters, whether as the occasion for a bold speculation and a bolder hope or as a remembered figure in history, would be a vastly impoverished Christianity, so unlike all which has hitherto been called Christianity that its further right to the term might be challenged. Many persons have concluded that historic Christianity, having served its day, is now to be superseded by other types of religious thought. If Christianity survives directly for another five hundred years we are quite safe in saying that its body of doctrine will be very different from that now held, even though the continuity of Christian experience may have been preserved from stage to stage. But whatever the issue, the general type of religious inquiry indicated by the Christological doctrines of the past will be perpetuated, since much that is meant by religion has been the occasion for those doctrines and has given them their substance.

Meanwhile a great deal of what is now being said and written on this subject is deliberately inadequate and evasive. In particular the historian who has been at work for a hundred years trying to recover the Jesus of the synoptic gospels has stood on his rights as a historian in refusing to consider any of those ultimate questions which piety has looked to the person of Jesus to answer. There is no denying that he has been warranted in so doing, since he is a historian and not a metaphysician, and historians in so far as they aspire to be scientists make a point of having no dealings with those final matters which lie beyond the restricted field of history. The resulting lives of Jesus have undoubtedly done much to recover the man who stood there at the dawn of the Christian era to mark its beginning and to give it its name. Yet religiously these books have been, as on their own ground they must be, disappointing. Their studied silences and careful avoidance of all those matters that enter into the Christological thought of the church leave us ill content. They do their dispassionate best to recover the historical figure, and having done so, they say, "Behold, the man." They do not go on to ask, much less to answer, the question which is in all our minds, whether this man can bear the superstructure of speculation which the centuries imposed upon him.

I have no slightest ambition to propose a modern Christology and am not competent to do so even had I the desire, being neither a metaphysician nor the son of a metaphysician. There seem to me to be, however, certain aspects of the situation which may be and indeed must be identified at the present time, as furnishing the premises of our thinking about the matter. These I offer without any necessary connection, and without any attempt to bring them together into a consistent whole, for what they may be worth to those who realize that since this is the field where apologetics is most active, here also we must be prepared for its gravest liabilities.

The title of this chapter was made deliberately ambiguous—the place of Jesus in his own religion. Is Christianity Jesus' own religion, and if so how? Liberal Christians have assumed that if it is not, it ought to be. Fundamentalists and the more radical critics agree that it is not and cannot be. Christianity, according to these latter, grew up as and still remains, not the religion which Jesus professed and practised, but a religion about him; he is thus the subject of the Christian religion. Historically I see no escape from this conclusion. Jesus was a Jew, and a devout Jew; he did not regard himself as a heretic founding a schismatic movement. Had he lived longer, it is conceivable that, like many religious reformers, he might have been forced out of the church of his day and compelled to organize a new movement. He was put to death before he had to make that decision; his disciples had to make it for him at a later time. We may not, however, indulge in speculations as to what Jesus might have done had he lived longer, since the one fact of which we are more certain than any other is his crucifixion under Pontius Pilate that cut short his work before its historical consequences had become plain to him. I see no escape, then, from the drastic historical judgment that Jesus was not a Christian, unless Christianity be simply reformed Judaism. Yet having said this it must be added at once that it is precisely this type of critical judgment which has made possible within Christianity all that we identify as most unlike Jesus, and that liberal Christianity has been right to insist that these endless perversions of the subject of our religion are a reproach. The poet would say that the church has used its fancy in creating its countless Christs rather than its imagination in telling the truth about Jesus, and that this is bad religious art.

The figure that has ruled Christian thought has been, however, Christ rather than Jesus. "Christ" is the account given of Jesus by persons who stood in the Jewish succession; it meant little or nothing to non-Jews and had to be replaced in Gentile Christianity by the term "Lord," and in the Nicene theology by "Logos—Word." All of these designations, and others, imply a prior idea of divinity or deity, with which Jesus was invested by his followers. The only one of them which he could possibly have accepted was that of "Christ—Messiah," and since we cannot be certain about his Messianic self-consciousness, whether he had any such self-consciousness and if so in what way he construed it, we are well within the facts in saying that the whole subsequent doctrine of the divinity of Jesus went far beyond anything that he claimed for himself; indeed, much of it the man of Galilee would not have understood and most of it he would have repudiated. Yet on the assumption that Jesus was not a Christian his followers have not exceeded their rights in making statements about him which he never would have made of himself. What matters here is honesty of thought; we may not find the full Nicene theology in embryo in the Gospels, waiting only to be matured in time. It is not there, and only an apologetic motive would incline any man to put it there by reading into a few proof texts meanings which they were not intended to bear.

Meanwhile the figure who has moved Christians is the Christ. In so far as this Christ was occasioned by and is to be identified with Jesus it has not been the historical man, but the cosmic figure who has influenced Christianity. This figure is not the result of wholly arbitrary and irrational processes of thought. Other historical figures have thus "belonged to the ages" through "the universalizing touch of death." No one questions the propriety of Tennyson's lines about Hallam:

> Strange friend, past, present, and to be;
> Loved deeper, darklier understood;
> Behold, I dream a dream of good,
> And mingle all the world with thee.

Much Christology is poetry of that sort, dealing with an experience not wholly different. This tendency to universalize persons whom we have known and loved is very deep rooted, and no one can say us nay when we so reconstrue our relation to them. It may well be that this is a truth of fact, and not merely memory comforting sorrow. The Christian desire to universalize Jesus was not irrational and is not unintelligible. Its primal impulse is strong and may be wholly valid. We cannot treat Christological speculation, at least in its promptings, as a unique and indefensible venture of Christian piety.

This universalized figure, however, always tends to lose its close connection with the historical person who was its first occasion and to become increasingly a creation of our own devising. "Christ" is the name which most Christians give to their own self-idealization, to all that they aspire to be and are not. Since innumerable Christs would be required to match the diversity of beliefs and ideals cherished by Christians, we can hardly believe in the objective existence of these many figures. When a man says that he believes in "the living Christ" he probably does not construe those words merely as a confidence in the immortality of Jesus of Nazareth. If it is this it is also something more, and that something more is a much closer approximation to his own circumstance and character. "The living Christ" would seem to be a name given to God, which carries with it an assurance that the God thus known as an inward presence is personal even as we are personal. The immortal Jesus, if ever known immediately, will probably prove to be a different person from this "living Christ" into whose making our own subjective contribution has gone.

Meanwhile it is this theological person, not the historical man, who has been the object of our Christian devotion. It has been "the Christ" who has mattered in Christianity and in so far as this term has done duty for the word "God" Christians have been right in giving their devotion to this universal divine person rather than to the man of history.

The historical study of the life of Jesus seems to have been prompted by a double motive. One of these motives is a disinterested historical desire to know the facts about the man. The Gospels are as legitimate a field for historical inquiry as any other subject-matter, and theology has neither the right nor the power to warn the historian off this field as ground too sacred to be invaded by the secular scholar. Indeed, the attempt to keep the historian off this ground is prompted by fear rather than confidence, and as such is not to be construed as a sign of strong faith. If we have faith in the man we shall not be afraid what the historian can do to him or to us. Disinterestedness, however, finds it hard to recover the man, for the simple reason that the sources require interpretation, and Schweitzer is probably right in despairing of a genuinely scientific life of Jesus. Here as elsewhere in the writing of history the recorded facts do not tell the whole of their story and the historian must risk his own contribution in order to call them into life. The dispassionate life of Jesus we may dismiss, therefore, as an unattainable scientific ideal. It is a question whether history can ever be written with perfect dispassionateness, certainly not in this instance. The greatest lives of Jesus, as Schweitzer says, have been written with love or hate, for hate can write that life as well as love.

The other motive which has prompted this historical study is an honest desire to correct the figures of "the living Christ" by the sources. This is a wholly commendable endeavor, since, as we have said, the tendency of that ideal character or idealized historical person is to lose its contact with the original who first inspired it and who is still supposed to warrant it. "The living Christ" ought not to give the lie to the historical Jesus, otherwise the term evaporates in the mists of pure romanticism. Unless "the living Christ" has some resemblance to the Jesus of history we are justified in dismissing the figure as pure mythology, useful, perhaps, as all religious myths have been useful, but without any guaranty in the outer world.

Yet the attempt to find in the historical Jesus a figure who shall relieve us of the responsibilities of a first-hand religious life fails. The Jesus of history cannot replace the Catholic Church or the infallible Protestant Bible as our seat of religious authority, since too much is left unsaid in the Gospels and there remains so much to say on our own account. Jesus never envisaged the modern twentieth-century Christian poring over the Gospels to find there a final answer to his questions of faith and conduct, and even had he envisaged such a possibility he would have refused the rôle which this reminiscent piety would now require him to play. For in his own time his silences to his disciples are too patent to allow us to believe that he would have accepted for countless later generations a responsibility which he refused to accept for his contemporaries. Jesus in his teaching seems to have gone with his disciples as far as they were able to go, yet he never took their lives out of their own hands. There seems to have been in him something of that same fear of disciples which other great prophets have known, not because he did not wish their loyalty, but because he feared the misconstructions to which it might be open. The honest answer to the question, "What would Jesus do?" is, in many instances, "We do not know." We may have very strong convictions as to his probable way of life, had his lot been cast in this time rather than in that time, yet we go beyond the facts when we refuse responsibility for our immediate Christian decisions on the ground that he has previously made the decision for us. He left us principles, but he did not give us rules sufficient to cover all the permutations and combinations of honest perplexity. The attempt to find in the teaching of Jesus a final seat of external authority is not only historically impossible; it is religiously ill-advised, since we have no reason to suppose that Jesus wished to turn the religious life from an original and even a creative endeavor into an imitation.

A friend of mine in England has recently published an honest book* in which he comes to the conclusion that the historical figure of Jesus cannot bear the weight of theological speculation imposed upon it, and that Christianity will greatly profit by ridding itself of the incubus of this speculation and by return-

* Frank Lenwood, *Jesus—Lord or Leader?* London, Constable and Co.

ing to the man himself. He doubts whether we are right to continue calling Jesus "Lord" and concludes that we should call him "Leader." I admire the book for its courage and am in accord with many of its conclusions, yet the title of the book seems to me an evasion of the real issue, since the term "Leader" carries with it some residual suggestion of the liberal hope that the teaching of Jesus may lift the responsibility for Christian living off our own shoulders. I should much prefer the terms "companion" or "friend" and believe them to be truer to experience. The Christian is one who has the right to believe that in the ultimate experiences of life, its temptations, its hopes, its sorrows and pains, he is not alone. He may be following where Jesus went before, but often he has to find the way for himself. Thomas Hardy comes close to our common experience when he says that Angel Clare, remembering the words of the Nazarene, "Let not your heart be troubled, neither let it be afraid," would have liked to confront Jesus and to have appealed to him to tell him his method. Not that the way of life as Jesus lived it may not be followed, but that going this way ought always to have, if it is to be a religious vocation, something of the quality of a first-hand experience. Harnack calls our attention to the fact that during all the earlier centuries there never was any deliberate imitation of

Christ; such imitation appears when the religion is in a period of stagnation and indecision. Copyists, here as elsewhere, abound only when creative work is in abeyance.

Moreover, the reconstruction of the person of the historical Jesus is not free from those dangers that accompany the fashioning of "the living Christ." In order to recover a living man from a remote past we must impute to him something of our own spirit as an act of interpretation. The failure of the best minds of a century of patient and professedly dispassionate study of the subject to reach any consistent agreement should discourage our passing over the direction of our lives to "some other man's dim thought of him," since we have no assurance that such thought is faithful to the original. And when we pass over the leadership of our lives to our own thought of him, it is well that we should realize the act of self-reliance that is inevitably involved.

In its own way the whole attempt to get back to the historical Jesus and to rest the case for religion upon his self-consciousness, his words and deeds, tends to make of such Christianity another monopoly, like that achieved by Calvinism. True, it is a much more humane and benevolent despotism that results, yet in its own way its effect is to deny man his rights in the relation and thus to destroy the religiousness of the relation. Could that ideal be achieved, yielding us a universally credible figure of the historical Jesus holding all power in heaven and on earth, a decline of religiousness would ensue. It is probably a good thing for Christianity that the state of the sources makes the realization of this ideal impossible and requires the risk of the interpretations which are implied in our personal accounts of the man. These historical difficulties create the permanent occasion for the indubitable quality of religiousness in the relation which exists when a man tries to follow Jesus.

A certain type of apologist delights to point out that each of the enduring world religions has looked to some historical man as its founder, and that Christianity, therefore, runs true to form in venerating Jesus. Since, however, it is an open question whether Jesus was the conscious and deliberate founder of the Christian religion, this veneration is not unambiguous. We would seem, thus, to honor him for doing what he never intended to do, instead of honoring him for what he himself was in his own time and person, a much more defensible practice.

Veneration for historical figures is a common custom with certain religions. It has at various times been made the whole substance of a religion, yet wherever we find this practice, as in the emperor worship of the Roman state, we regard it as a very meager and imperfect kind of religion. It is hard to see why a practice which we hold to be inadequate in other instances should be treated as an exception in the case of Christianity. Only an apologetic motive could incline us to make this exception and to point to the practice of hero-worship elsewhere as warranting this worship in Christianity. Moreover, few founders of historical religions have ever been identified with God to the degree that Christian thought has identified the substances of the Son and the Father. I see little or no help to be had from this analogy, since beyond the similarity there is the Christian differentia.

A liberal type of apologetic has latterly been telling us that while we are agnostic as regards God, we are gnostic as regards Jesus and therefore may say at least this, that God must be as good as Jesus is. The doctrine of the divinity of Christ is thus metamorphosed into a doctrine of the Christlikeness of God. Indeed, Professor McGiffert has written a serious study of primitive Christian thought in defense of the thesis that the early Christians had little or no interest in the God of the cosmos, and that

Christ was "The God of the Early Christians," to whom the creator was later accommodated.

The contemporary form of this logic, that God must be as good as Jesus is, may seem at first a plausible and attractive way of stating the Christological case. Yet, for myself, I have never been able to suppress the suspicion that there lingers about this statement a strong strain of the apologetic motive. The man who holds this position is trying to save a doctrine; he is not working—in Wordsworth's phrase—with his eye fixed at all times steadily upon the subject.

This account of the matter concedes our agnosticism in the presence of the cosmic mystery, yet instantly takes away the sting of that agnosticism by our Christian gnosticism. This does not seem a wholly candid mental transaction, for problems are not real to which we have the answer in advance. Furthermore, Christians have never said that apart from Christ we are wholly agnostic about God. They have always said, and said truly, that men before Christ knew a great deal about God, and that God has never left the world without witness to himself. If there is one recorded saying of Jesus which he certainly did not say it is that in the Fourth Gospel, to the effect that all who came before him were thieves and robbers. That statement is utterly unlike the Jesus of the first three Gospels and denies the whole drift of the synoptic teaching. So we have to-day much reliable knowledge of our universe which does not derive from Jesus, and this knowledge cannot be denied or ignored. We shall never stop the valid work of the sciences with this type of Christology.

Furthermore, this particular bit of apologetics has the effect of making us quite content with our initial agnosticism, and no religion encourages a man to be content with agnosticism. A complacent agnosticism invites sloth and indifference before the mysteries that surround us, and the secret persuasion that we know the answer in advance makes us careless in sharing in the normal and right endeavor of the human mind to penetrate the mystery. Browning says somewhere that the acknowledgment of God in Christ solves for us all questions in the universe. That is a gross overstatement of the fact. The acknowledgment of God in Christ may encourage us to place a particular interpretation upon many of the processes of nature and history, but it simply does not answer countless questions that the human mind must ask and for which it must try to find an answer. I write down this reversed doctrine of the divinity of Christ, that God must be at least as good as Jesus is, as too patently apologetic and too complacently in-

different to the honest brain work of the world to
be of any permanent help.

Christological speculation in general seems to be
addressed to a profound idea—namely, that religion
ought to come fully true in a human experience, that
there must be some windward point where God and
man are not set over against each other, but are at
one. The traditional Christology of the church, so
construed, voices the conviction that we have such a
fulfilled religious fact in the person of Jesus.

As such it must always remain one of the boldest
and most comprehensive attempts at religious statement that history knows. As one reviews the history
of the Christological controversies of the fourth and
fifth centuries one is struck by two facts; first, that
the positions eventually declared to be heretical are
in every instance simpler and more intelligible than
the orthodox position; second, that the orthodox
position is always a paradox. The heretics were constantly stressing one of the natures of Christ to the
neglect or detriment of the other. Their accounts of
him were consistent and any of the heresies is easier
to understand and accept than the orthodox doctrine.
This doctrine is, however, not so much a compromise
as an endeavor to comprehend all the factors in the
situation, even though they seem to involve an initial

contradiction. It has been said that Christianity owes its survival to its inclination to try to compass contradictions, more than to any other single trait in its thought. This tendency appears most clearly in the Christological controversies and the resulting Chalcedonian Definition of the two natures in the one person.

We spoke in the last chapter of the religious maturity of Pascal's thought. He carries this maturity into his reflections upon Jesus. His words are bold, with the boldness of an Irenæus or an Athanasius; they must disturb many a timid pietist in our own time, yet they seem to me to come very near the secret of all Christology. "Faith," says Pascal, "embraces many truths which seem contradictory. The source of this is the union of the two natures in Jesus Christ. The source of all heresies is the exclusion of some of these truths. Men before Jesus did not know . . . if they were great or little. The two natures which are in the righteous man . . . are the two worlds, and a member and image of Jesus Christ. Two natures in Jesus Christ, two advents, two states of human nature. I consider Jesus Christ in all persons and in ourselves."

These stray sentences, which play over Pascal's scene like shafts of lightning in the darkness, prove the profoundly religious quality of his Christology.

To his thinking Jesus compassed and vindicated in a single experience all that we mean by religion. The formal doctrine of his natures is simply an elaboration of the paradox of religion set at rest for the moment in the character of Jesus.

I have previously said that the life and words of Jesus seem to lack that tension which comes from too one-sided accounts of religion, and that the equipoise of his mind gives to his dual thought of God and man a very great and rare maturity. The want of a sense of sin, as it is commonly called, is not so much a tacit assertion of ethical self-assurance as the absence of any radical discrepancy felt to exist between himself as subject and God his father as object. In the want of this felt discrepancy it is fair to say that he had, to this extent, a divine self-consciousness. Yet this is not so much what he thought about himself as what he thought of the ultimate nature of the religious relation between God and man. That, at least is what the bolder Christian thought holds out to all of us as our goal. We are not to refuse for ourselves what we think we discover in Jesus, and what the formal doctrine accords him, these two natures in one person.

There is I think, therefore, sound historical warrant for much of the Christological speculation of the centuries, and I believe this speculation to be addressed directly to the paradox of the religious consciousness and as such to be of permanent significance. This whole reconsideration of the historic doctrine along the lines indicated by Pascal's striking sentences needs elaboration. The difficulty with Christology in its conventional forms is that we assume it to be a truth to be told only of Jesus and not pertinent for ourselves. All that makes Jesus "unique" in this respect and puts him either on the side of the divine monopoly or among the curious mutations of history which have had no counterpart or consequence, takes away from our thought about the two natures in Jesus Christ its permanent religious significance. The whole weight of Christian argument in this matter points in one direction. What was true in Jesus and of Jesus ought to be and may be true in us and of us.

Simple Christian piety has found in Jesus what the artists call "a concrete universal," as against an abstract universal. The difficulty with most of our thought about life and the world today is just this abstractness, which we owe to the generalizing habits of mind bred in us by discipline in the sciences. Scientists are interested, it is true, in particular objects, but only as they may be made to yield general laws. After the general law has been elicited the scientist's interest in the particular ceases. We all know the medical specialist who has an initial interest in the case, and then little or no interest in the patient after the case has been identified and dealt with in the routine way. He is occupied with particular forms of human suffering, but not with the concrete sufferer. His scientific training has killed the artist in him. There is altogether too much of this thinking in our time, and religion is undoubtedly suffering from our habit of dealing with it as a set of generalizations. God himself tends to become an abstraction, a compendium of laws.

Now Christianity has greatly profited in the past because Christian devotion, expressing itself artistically rather than scientifically, has seen universal meanings in the concrete figure of Jesus. The universal is not evaporated away in the form of psychological and moral laws, leaving a discarded historical particular in whom we have no further interest. The interest and worth remain in the concrete person, and Christian art asks only to see further into the mystery of the individual who is its constant subject.

An abstract theology can never tell us the whole truth or intimate the most significant truth of Jesus; since the generalizations elicited from him have no reality, they are merely modes of our thinking. I am persuaded that Christology needs to stop going to school to science and to go to school again to art, in order to understand itself. Our failure to understand how art finds the realities of things is responsible for our present scepticism as to the value of any theory of the person of Christ. If we could see the world as artists see it, our approach to Jesus would be religiously more accurate and adequate.

For myself I can conceive of no Christianity without Jesus Christ. He has entered, both as a remembered person in history and as the occasion for bold speculation, far too deeply into our thought to be dismissed easily. Nor can I conceive of any religion of the future which will not make its reckoning and its peace with him. What he did and said has now become a necessary part of man's way of thinking about religion and of living a religious life. If he does not control that life autocratically, he companions it constantly in memory and imagination. We need not feel, however, that this sense that our lives are involved with his commits us to the specific theological formulas which centuries ago were employed to interpret and to vindicate him. For he is greater than his apologists and does not look to their defense for his immortality in history. The Gospels give us a strong impression of one who was not dependent on any temporal suffrage for his religious life. He does not need in after-centuries an apologia which was plainly superfluous in his own day. The closer one seems to come to the man himself the more impertinent and irrelevant conventional apologetics become. We should have the courage and the generosity to go as far as is historically possible in letting him stand in his own right and speak his own words, whether we hear or whether we forbear. That is the only useful Christian apologetic.

One last word. Jesus of Nazareth plainly had but one desire—to turn men to God. If the synoptic tradition is to be trusted, and it is the only source we have upon which we can rely in these matters, he did not wish men's thoughts and devotions to stop at himself. He was aware of the danger of this and seems at all times to have been anxious to pass men's thoughts beyond himself to his Father. The words, "Why callest thou me good?" which have given such trouble to those who defend the dogma of his sinlessness, are probably not to be construed in a purely ethical sense. Jesus was here refusing to let men's minds rest on him when they should rest on God.

So, St. Paul does not hesitate to say that we are Christ's, but he does not fail to add that Christ is God's. And he looks for a time when Christ shall have delivered up his kingdom to God the Father, that God may be all in all. Any Christology that stops short of this consummation, or is content with less, must be inadequate. In so far as we come into any contact with the mind of Christ we are compelled to think of God and to seek God. There was a holy urgency in the life of Jesus passing on the loyalty of men as devotion to God, directing it toward God, ill content if that devotion could be satisfied with less; as there is also in the logic of formal Christo-logical thought the same movement.

We cannot believe that any doctrine of Christ which is today merely a shelter from the imperious mystery of things, a halfway house along the road, meets what is the true impulse of Christological thought. We must believe that Jesus, were he our contemporary, would not invite us to come apart and tarry with him in some intellectual seclusion; his mind would be going on its way today and tomorrow and the day following. Luther said that when Jesus was here on earth he did not live a secluded life, he lived openly and among men. He had then, as he certainly would have now, an intuitive trust in God, but he would not have ignored or disparaged the effort to know more about the divine mystery.

Our doctrine of Christ, whatever it may be, if it is

to be faithful to the original, cannot, then, become the warrant for a studied indifference to the thoughts of men in the presence of their world; it must be our invitation to enter into that "Eternity of Thought" which is the being of God.